OECD Digital Government Studies

Digital Government in Mexico

SUSTAINABLE AND INCLUSIVE TRANSFORMATION

This document, as well as any data and map included herein, are without prejudice to the status of or sovereignty over any territory, to the delimitation of international frontiers and boundaries and to the name of any territory, city or area.

The statistical data for Israel are supplied by and under the responsibility of the relevant Israeli authorities. The use of such data by the OECD is without prejudice to the status of the Golan Heights, East Jerusalem and Israeli settlements in the West Bank under the terms of international law.

Please cite this publication as:
OECD (2020), *Digital Government in Mexico: Sustainable and Inclusive Transformation*, OECD Digital Government Studies, OECD Publishing, Paris, *https://doi.org/10.1787/6db24495-en*.

ISBN 978-92-64-41712-0 (print)
ISBN 978-92-64-55068-1 (pdf)
ISBN 978-92-64-54684-4 (HTML)
ISBN 978-92-64-31497-9 (epub)

OECD Digital Government Studies
ISSN 2413-1954 (print)
ISSN 2413-1962 (online)

Photo credits: Cover © Prospera Digital/Mi Salud (Image provided by the Ministry of Public Administration, Mexico)

Corrigenda to publications may be found on line at: *www.oecd.org/about/publishing/corrigenda.htm*.
© OECD 2020

The use of this work, whether digital or print, is governed by the Terms and Conditions to be found at *http://www.oecd.org/termsandconditions*.

Foreword

This review of Digital Government in Mexico discusses and assesses the evolution, achievements and challenges of the digital government policy in Mexico. It was prepared at the request of the Coordination of the National Digital Strategy office (Coordinación de la Estrategia Digital Nacional, CEDN) at the Office of the President in Mexico with the support of the Ministry of Public Administration (Secretaría de la Función Pública, SFP), and the Research and Innovation Centre on Information and Communications Technology (INFOTEC). The review provides recommendations on how to strengthen the governance and accelerate the digital transformation of the public sector in Mexico.

Since the early 2000s, Mexico has sought to make the most of digital opportunities to improve government performance. It first partnered with the OECD in the 2005 eGovernment Review of Mexico. In 2011, the OECD Public Governance Review of Mexico also touched upon the implementation of e-government.

Mexico has engaged closely with the OECD on open government data, which is a critical element for the digital transformation. The 2016 Open Government Data Review of Mexico was followed by the 2018 report on Open Government Data in Mexico: The Way Forward. The collaboration with Mexico was also pivotal for the development of the 2017 OECD/G20 "Compendium of good practices on the use of open data for anti-corruption".

These continuous efforts have borne fruit. Mexico has established itself as a global and regional leader in digital government and open government data. However, as digital government matures and requires alignment across policy areas, more effective co ordination will be needed from the centre to ensure coherent and cohesive digital transformation across the entire public sector. This is a core element of the OECD Recommendation of the Council on Digital Government Strategies adopted in 2014. Open, collaborative and inclusive approaches require a cultural change in the administration, and the right leadership and political support to overcome institutional legacies and silos. These fundamental changes require a governance framework that links and engages the different actors for a sustainable implementation of digital government strategies and secures long-term continuity and sustainability of actions and results.

The current volume of Digital Government in Mexico takes stock of Mexico's journey towards the digital transformation of government. It focuses on a whole-of-government approach and on sound governance frameworks as enablers of sustained policy results. It looks at the provision of public services that use data and emerging technologies, and involve the users in service design processes. It acknowledges successes and identifies the areas of opportunity (for instance, in terms of governance) that will help sustain the emergence of Mexico as a global digital leader.

This report contributes to and benefits from the OECD Going Digital project, an OECD wide two-year initiative assessing the impact of the digital revolution across policy areas. It also draws on the strengths of OECD policy communities in this area, including the OECD Working Party of Senior Digital Government Officials (E-Leaders).

Acknowledgements

This report was prepared by the OECD Directorate for Public Governance, under the leadership of Marcos Bonturi.

The report was produced by the OECD Reform of Public Sector Division, headed by Stéphane Jacobzone, Acting Head of Division. It has benefited from the strategic orientation and revisions of Barbara-Chiara Ubaldi, Acting Deputy Head of the OECD Reform of Public Sector Division and lead of the Digital Transformation of the Public Sector work.

The report was drafted by Jacob Arturo Rivera Perez, Digital Government and Open Data Policy Analyst, Reform of Public Sector, OECD; and Rodrigo Mejia Ricart, digital government policy consultant. The authors are grateful to Raquel Páramo and Javier González for administrative support and Liv Gaunt for editorial assistance.

The report has benefited from the expertise of the OECD Working Party of Senior Digital Government Officials (E-Leaders). This project would not have been possible without the support of the Coordination of the National Digital Strategy at the Office of the President in Mexico; the Ministry of Public Administration; and the Research and Innovation Centre on Information and Communications Technology.

Finally, the Secretariat would like to acknowledge the invaluable contribution of Yolanda Martinez, Coordinator of the National Digital Strategy, Mexico; Alejandra Lagunes, former Coordinator of the National Digital Strategy, Mexico; and Tania Paola Cruz Romero, Head of the Digital Government Unit of the Ministry of Public Administration and their teams. The OECD Secretariat is deeply thankful to Ambassador Mónica Aspe, Permanent Representative of Mexico to the OECD, and Maya Camacho, Second Secretary from the Permanent Delegation of Mexico to the OECD, for all their support throughout this project.

Table of contents

Foreword	3
Acknowledgements	5
Executive summary	9
Assessment and Recommendations	11
The fourth industrial revolution: Leveraging digital government in Mexico	12
Governance for sustainable and inclusive digital government	13
Strides towards a digital and user-driven administration in Mexico	19
Building digital capability in the Mexican public sector	21
References	24
Notes	25
1 The case for a digital government in Mexico	27
The age of disruption	28
Digital government at the core of public sector reform	29
References	31
Note	32
2 The evolution from e-government to digital government in Mexico	33
References	37
3 Governance for sustainable and inclusive digital government	39
The National Digital Strategy (2013-18)	40
Political leadership: Creating an enabling environment for change	50
Organisational frameworks to deliver on digital ambitions	52
References	53
Notes	55
4 Strides towards a digital and user-driven administration in Mexico	57
Digital service transformation	58
A data culture that supports digital strategy and delivery	60
Building digital capability in the Mexican public sector	64
References	68
Notes	70

Figures

Figure 1. Structure of the Mexican National Digital Strategy: Objectives and enablers	13
Figure 2. OECD fixed broadband subscriptions per 100 inhabitants, by technology, December 2017	14
Figure 1.1. The digital transformation of the public sector	31
Figure 3.1. Structure of the Mexican National Digital Strategy: Objectives and enablers	41
Figure 3.2. Mexico's performance in international indices on digital government	41
Figure 3.3. Internet users as share of the total population	42
Figure 3.4. Mobile subscriptions per 100 inhabitants	43
Figure 3.5. OECD fixed broadband subscriptions per 100 inhabitants, by technology, December 2017	43
Figure 3.6. OECD mobile broadband subscriptions per 100 inhabitants, by technology, December 2017	44
Figure 3.7. Results of the 2018 OECD Open Government Data Review of Mexico: General summary	49
Figure 4.1. The transformation of the administrative procedures required by heirs when confronted with the death of their parents	61
Figure 4.2. Data governance in the public sector	64

Boxes

Box 1. Proposals for action	18
Box 2. Proposals for action	23
Box 2.1. 2005 e-Government Study of Mexico: Key policy recommendations	36
Box 2.2. Public Governance Review of Mexico of 2011:	37
Box 3.1. Leveraging new technologies to foster inclusion with Prospera Digital	45
Box 3.2. Carpeta Ciudadana (citizen file): Enhancing data management and service delivery in Spain	46
Box 3.3. Digitalisation agencies in Portugal and Denmark	52
Box 4.1. Gob.mx: Transforming service delivery and digital engagement in Mexico	59
Box 4.2. BlockchainHackMX: Building blockchain capability in Mexico	59
Box 4.3. Transforming service delivery in Korea through life-events approaches	61
Box 4.4. France: The Villani Report	62
Box 4.5. Attracting new talent in government in the United States	65
Box 4.6. 18F's agile procurement agreements in the United States	67

Follow OECD Publications on:

 http://twitter.com/OECD_Pubs

 http://www.facebook.com/OECDPublications

 http://www.linkedin.com/groups/OECD-Publications-4645871

 http://www.youtube.com/oecdilibrary

 http://www.oecd.org/oecddirect/

Executive summary

The digital transformation is bringing disruptive change for the economies, societies and public sectors across OECD countries. An unprecedented wave of technological change is affecting the structures and organisations of both businesses and public administrations. Governments have to anticipate, embrace and manage this transformation if they do not want to be outpaced, provide outdated services or run the risk of policy failures. Public sector organisations need to be able to provide services and solutions that match citizens' expectations if they want to maintain or reinforce public trust.

Mexico must to continue to integrate digital tools and approaches into the fabric of the state to become more agile, open and responsive as it adapts to an age of digital disruption.

This report raises questions and provides policy recommendations to help Mexico achieve further progress in digital government. In particular, it underscores the importance of a governance framework that supports sustained and sustainable policies to benefit Mexican citizens and bolster public trust.

With a growing broad understanding of the implications of digitalisation for government and the public sector, Mexico has engaged with the OECD to make its digital ambitions a reality. The office for Coordination of the National Digital Strategy, within the Office of the President, and the Ministry of Public Administration have played a key role in providing leadership. Since 2012, Mexico has delivered results in line with the objectives of the National Digital Strategy. The positive outcomes of initiatives such as Gob.mx (the central public service delivery portal) and Próspera Digital (a digital inclusion programme) have paid off. The achievements in terms of the open data policy are reflected in Mexico's fifth place ranking in the 2017 edition of the OECD Open, Useful and Re-usable data (OURdata) Index, and are clear proof of how policy investments have delivered results.

The digital transformation of the Mexican public sector should remain a priority to secure enhanced efforts and greater benefits for Mexican citizens. Maintaining an effective governance framework will be crucial for avoiding setbacks caused by inaction. Like other countries, Mexico needs to ensure the right leadership and governance arrangements to sustain and accelerate digitalisation efforts and avoid being left behind as OECD countries move ahead in the digital transformation of their public sectors.

Key policy recommendations

- Empower digital transformation officers within public sector organisations, in particular by exploring options to establish closer working relations between them and the political leadership of their organisation.
- Drawing upon the example of the Commission for the Development of e Government (CIDGE), which brings together IT directors from public sector institutions, establish a high-level collegial body to provide strategic direction and co-ordination of digital government with key issues of relevance for the National Digital Strategy. This body should be responsible for addressing the increasingly politically sensitive questions that surround the digital transformation of the public

sector and ensure that the implementation is aligned with the broader digital agenda and the government's strategic policy objectives.

- Consider setting up an agency for digital transformation attached to an institution with the necessary political clout (e.g. the President's Office or the Ministry of Finance), while ensuring it has adequate independence, mandate, power and resources for sustainable success and long-term continuity.
- Review standards, design principles, guidelines and other tools to make sure they foster more joined-up approaches to service delivery.
- Demonstrate the value of data as a strategic asset for business operations inside the public administration working with the different public sector organisations.
- Develop a strategy for acquiring new talent in critical areas and bringing the skills of the existing public sector workforce in line with the needs for the digital transformation.
- Clarify digital, data, and ICT roles and competency frameworks in the public sector.
- Review talent acquisition frameworks to provide fit-for-purpose commissioning environments for hiring external technical talent for specific projects with an agile approach.
- Review business cases methods and ICT commissioning frameworks to ensure that they support agile contracting, collaboration and joined-up digital delivery models.

Assessment and Recommendations

This section analyses the current digital government landscape in Mexico and outlines proposed recommendations.

The statistical data for Israel are supplied by and under the responsibility of the relevant Israeli authorities. The use of such data by the OECD is without prejudice to the status of the Golan Heights, East Jerusalem and Israeli settlements in the West Bank under the terms of international law.

The fourth industrial revolution: Leveraging digital government in Mexico

The age of disruption

The world is facing an age of unique technological change. The speed, depth and breadth of this change are reshaping economies and societies across the globe. New business models are upending entire industries. Technology companies are taking over as the world's most valuable firms, autonomous vehicles are taking the streets, distributed models challenge incumbents and the Internet of Things (IoT) is making digital cities a reality. All this is already changing how we live, work and relate to one another. Still, more innovation is to be expected as our ability to produce, store and process massive amounts of data accelerates.

Governments around the world have no option but to adjust to this pace of change. Understanding how to leverage emerging technologies to reshape responses to changing expectations about public services, and building the capabilities to respond to this changing environment, are priorities for policy makers. Public authorities have become aware of the need to build digital capacity, update governance arrangements and transform business processes to meet the challenges of the 21st century and overcome traditional models that too often rely on outsourcing digital skills and capability. Analogue governments cannot effectively serve digital economies and societies, which require governments to be digital.

The digital disruption has barely started, and it is likely to accelerate. Deprioritising the digital transformation of the public sector or overseeing the current and upcoming challenges could drive significant failures in the Mexican public sector. This study seeks to flag these potential pitfalls for the Mexican government and encourage constructive and informed policy action going forward.

Digital government at the core of public sector reform

Unprecedented levels of home-based and mobile connectivity enable new public service delivery arrangements that are more convenient and that allow for data and user-driven continuous improvement, while saving time and resources for users and the public sector. Beginning in the late 1990s, governments strived to implement e-government – "the use of information and communication technologies (ICTs), and particularly the Internet, to achieve better government" (OECD, 2014). The e-government wave had a number of shortcomings. Most notably, it left a legacy of siloed systems, digital fragmentation and the digitisation of services without significant transformation – from processes to organisational culture.

These outcomes and new levels of technological development led the OECD to call for a paradigm shift in the use of technology in the public sector, encouraging governments to move from e-government to digital government (OECD, 2014). Digital government uses technology to enable open, user-driven, proactive and inclusive public services; redesign government processes; and take data-driven decisions (OECD, forthcoming). It also enables the rise of government as a platform, facilitates greater integration of services, as well as deeper collaboration and sharing within and outside of the public sector.

Mexico's efforts to achieve digital government in the past few decades cannot be neglected. In particular, the push for digitalisation, driven by the Coordination of the National Digital Strategy at the Office of the President, has achieved significant success. Today, roughly 90% of government transactions can be initiated on line and 75% can be completed digitally (IDB, 2018). Nevertheless, only 10% of Mexicans reported completing their last government transaction through digital channels, and government transactions often require several interactions to be completed. To reap the full benefits of digital government, Mexico might benefit from adopting an increasingly multi-channel, joined-up and user driven approach, which can affect societal well-being and hence support increased public trust in government.

Governance for sustainable and inclusive digital government

The evolution from e-government to digital government in Mexico

A new National Digital Strategy (Estrategia Digital Nacional, EDN) was launched in Mexico under the 2012-18 federal administration, providing a clear articulation with the public sector reform programme and the National Development Plan. The Coordination of the National Digital Strategy was established under the Office of the President to oversee and co ordinate its implementation.

The EDN, its structure and objectives have a significant focus on improving public sector performance (Government of Mexico, 2013). The EDN identified five strategic objectives that would drive the digital transformation of government, education, health, the economy and government-citizen relations (Figure 1). These objectives are supported by five key enablers: 1) connectivity; 2) digital skills and inclusion; 3) interoperability; 4) legal framework; and 5) open data.

Figure 1. Structure of the Mexican National Digital Strategy: Objectives and enablers

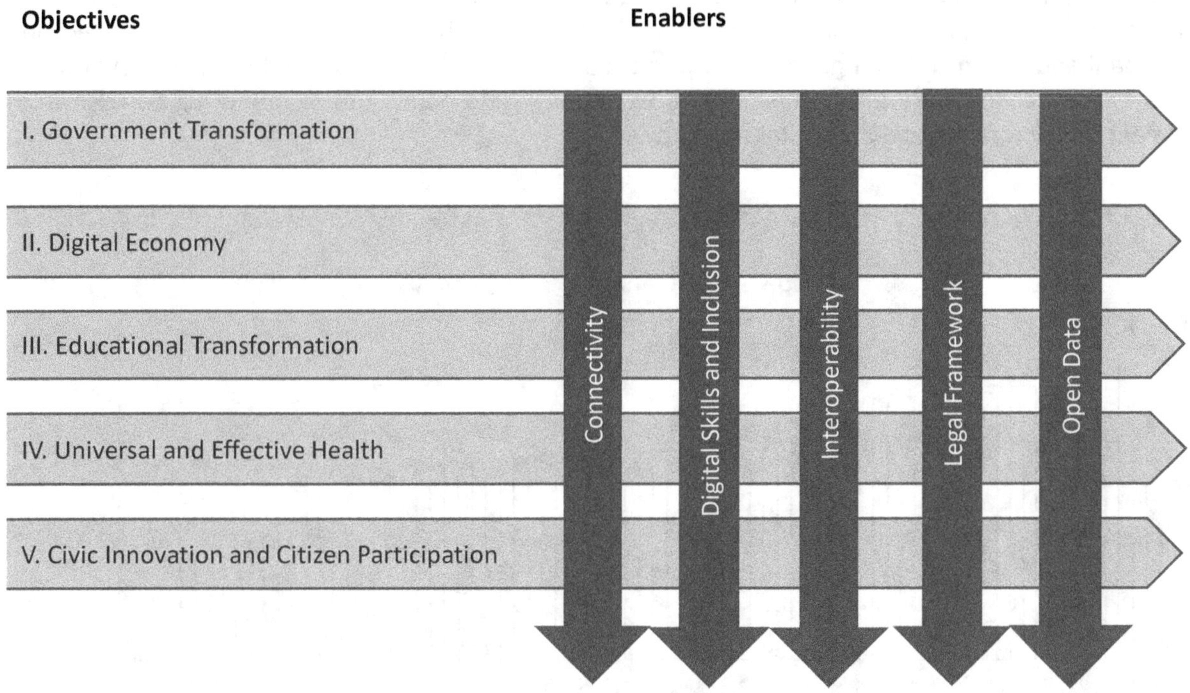

Objectives
- I. Government Transformation
- II. Digital Economy
- III. Educational Transformation
- IV. Universal and Effective Health
- V. Civic Innovation and Citizen Participation

Enablers
- Connectivity
- Digital Skills and Inclusion
- Interoperability
- Legal Framework
- Open Data

Source: Government of Mexico (2013) Estrategia Nacional Digital.

Mexico identified early on the power of digital and the country has firmly established itself as a leader in Latin America and the Caribbean and, progressively, the world, as its performance in international metrics show. Mexico ranks 23rd in the UN's Online Service Index, up from 35th in 2014, and 5th in the OECD Open, Useful and Re-Usable Data (OURData) Index, up from 10th in 2014.

However, success should not lead to complacency, as experience proves that digital initiatives often fail and the implementation of digital strategies does not always lead to the desired results (Bughin et al., 2018). The digital transformation of government entails a continuous evolution, which demands sustained effort. As governments operate in political environments of competing interests and changing policy priorities, a solid governance framework is essential to secure continuity for the effective implementation of strategies and sustained long-term results. Effective governance in the 21st century needs to support governments capable to embed new ways of working and advanced analytics into public sector operations at all levels to draw on new insights, enable smart automation where valuable, and develop new business models in order to make public policy and service delivery more effective.

The enablers of the digital transformation

Connectivity

Access to basic ICT infrastructure, and notably the Internet, is the backbone of the digital revolution. With an overall performance below the OECD average – due to a relatively low share of the population using in the Internet – in 2013 Mexico took bold, courageous action to address this challenge and accelerate the country's actions to establish the environment needed to transition to the digital economy. Most remarkably, access to the Internet and broadband was recognised as a constitutional right for all Mexicans as of June 2013, thus putting pressure on public authorities to live up to this standard. While Mexico still scores below the OECD average, it has experienced significant growth in the number of Internet users in the country, particularly after 2014.

While these are encouraging results, Mexico still lags far behind OECD peers in the development and adoption of critical infrastructure for the digital transformation, such as access to and use of fixed and mobile broadband. From a digital government perspective, Mexico would do well to double down on its efforts to expand connectivity and inclusion as it would allow the country to reap the full benefits from government transformation and the digital economy.

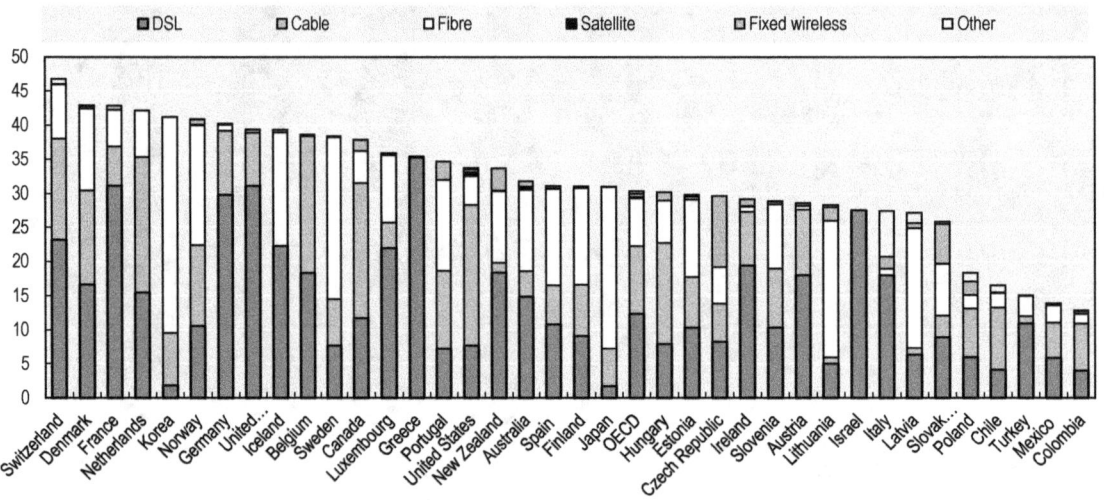

Figure 2. OECD fixed broadband subscriptions per 100 inhabitants, by technology, December 2017

Note: Canada: Fixed wireless includes satellite. France: cable includes VDSL2 THD. Germany: cable includes HFC lines; fibre includes fibre lines provided by cable operators; fixed wireless includes BWA subscribers; other includes leased lines. Israel: temporary OECD estimates. Italy: terrestrial fixed wireless data include WiMax lines; other includes vDSL services. Switzerland and United States: data for December 2017 are estimates. Information on data for Israel: http://oe.cd/israel-disclaimer.
Source: OECD Broadband Portal, www.oecd.org/sti/broadband/oecdbroadbandportal.htm.

Digital skills and inclusion

The EDN also points out digital inclusion and the development of digital skills as a critical factor making digital success possible in the country. Indeed, building the digital skills of society can help drive innovation in the production of goods and services and their adoption, use and consumption by members of society.

Mexico has set up important initiatives, such as MéxicoX, an online learning platform with over 230 courses for specialised and academic training for teachers, benefiting more than 1.5 million users (OECD, 2018a). Similarly, @prende.mx has provided schools with technological equipment and a knowledge-sharing platform for teachers on using technology as part of the learning process, and has run pilots aimed at improving students' access to digital technologies and the responsible use of the Internet.

While these initiatives are promising, they still have shortcomings that need to be addressed. @prende.mx has yet to develop indicators of success to understand its impact on broader education outcomes or skills development. Moreover, it is unclear whether the measures taken are sufficient to instil a digital culture among teachers. Finally, it seems that not enough attention is paid to low-skilled workers that will increasingly face pressures to upskill and reskill. The rise of automation makes this all the more relevant and urgent. The transition towards broad automation may after all take place more rapidly than we expect.

Interoperability

Mexico has focused on enhancing interoperability as a driver of government business processes and service transformation. The Mexican single portal, Gob.mx, with the support of a new normative framework for digital government, has been driving interoperability between government departments. In addition, the initiative InteroperaMX has been an outstanding achievement for facilitating data sharing within the public sector.

InteroperaMX, inspired by the Estonian X-Road, is a platform that allows public institutions to securely share reliable and trustworthy data, with clear identification of the source and certification of the information. This effort, launched in 2016 and operational as of 2018, is driven by the vision of a public administration where the user only has to provide information once to the public sector.

The initiative to advance interoperability in the country is of a critical strategic importance, as it is a structural enabler to achieve end-to-end digital services and seamless government. A seamless government would significantly reshape how the public administration operates, including between levels of government, to better serve citizens and become more agile.

The birth certificate is the use case chosen by the government to illustrate the power of InteroperaMX and thus of interoperability in the public sector. A birth certificate is required as proof of a citizen's identity for 46% of all government transactions at the federal level. Moreover, 45% of completed government transactions in Mexico concern proofs of identity and civil registration (IDB, 2018). These initiatives have enormous potential to drive transformation both within the public sector in Mexico and outside of it by enabling digital delivery models. However, they so far lack scale. Only a limited number of public services have adopted these solutions as a means to achieve interoperability. In addition, these solutions do not provide users with full transparency on the use and sharing of personal data by public institutions. This final point is one that could and should be considered for future iterations.

Legal framework

The legal and regulatory framework for digital government and information and communications technologies is an inevitable component of the governance framework that needs to be adjusted in line with the needs of the digital age. Mexico has also taken significant steps in this domain. As previously mentioned, access to the Internet has now become a constitutional right. The Mexican government has focused important energies on fostering competition in the telecommunications sector under the 2012-18

Peña Nieto administration. It has also pushed for the modernisation of the regulatory and normative framework for digital government.

The current legal and regulatory framework of digital government in Mexico provides a vision for the progressive digital integration of the federal public administration. Furthermore, the legal framework of ICT procurement, digital identification and signature, and personal data protection have recently been modernised.

These changes should be welcomed and encouraged as they facilitate more joined-up and data-driven approaches in the implementation of digital government. However, more is needed for these approaches to be streamlined and ingrained in the fabric of government as default ways of working. As the government of Mexico seeks to enhance service delivery through digital approaches, it seems of critical importance that frameworks such as those dedicated to ICT commissioning are revised or complemented to facilitate agile contracting and development.

Open government data

Data, including open government data (OGD), is a strategic enabler of the digital transformation that allows government to work as a platform for the co-creation of public value (OECD, 2018c). Open-by-default standards give governments the opportunity to leverage outside talent and capabilities not only to help advance government accountability, but also public sector performance and social and economic innovations that deliver convenient new services and promote well-being (OECD, forthcoming).

In 2016, the government of Mexico, through the Coordination of the National Digital Strategy, the General Direction of Open Data and the Ministry of Public Administration partnered with the OECD to perform an OECD Open Government Data Review of Mexico (OECD, 2018b). The review provided an assessment of open government data policies in Mexico in the light of the OECD analytical framework for open government data (Ubaldi, 2013) and highlighted opportunities for Mexico to reap the full benefits of OGD to support the digital transformation of Mexico.

The Open Government Data Review of Mexico benefited from a follow up project in 2018 to assess the progress made since the review. The 2018 report also assessed the present environment to make forward-looking recommendations that would help the government of Mexico make strategic choices today so that the national OGD ecosystem continues to grow in maturity and robustness (OECD, 2018b). The conclusions of this OECD report remain valid to this date.

Political leadership: Creating an enabling environment for change

International experiences highlight that transforming government requires the mobilisation of a myriad of actors, networks, structures and systems, which demands substantial political capability. Because of these requirements in terms of political leverage, digital government authorities are very often located at a central department or ministry, close or within the centre of government, with a transversal mandate such as a finance minister, public administration minister or cabinet office, which is consistent with Mexico's experience.

Mexico has successfully adopted a model where the political push comes from the centre, via the Coordination of the National Digital Strategy located in the Office of the President, with the implementing drive and support coming from the Ministry of Public Administration. Measured by the rate of digitalisation of public services, this model has delivered. Mexico has consolidated itself as a regional leader when it comes to the level of digitalisation of government transactions (IDB, 2018; OECD, 2018a). However, the model is not without its shortcomings.

One key weakness of the current Mexican model is that a disproportionate level of the political drive – and thus the ability to exert influence across sectors – depends on the individual executives within the Office of the President, who might often struggle to find the time required to effectively steer the digitalisation agenda (Bracken and Greenway, 2018). Experience shows that while digital agendas operated from the centre of government can be extremely effective, they also risk becoming too closely associated with a specific executive or political leader, whereas digital government does not have a political colour. The existing model provides no certain answer for the need of sustained efforts in digital government implementation, with the risk for the digital agenda to lose relevance because of political elections.

Several of the most digitally advanced OECD countries have attempted to solve this tension by creating a more stable institutional set up with a co-ordinating mandate – e.g. ranging from a specialised agency for digitalisation headed by a senior executive reporting directly to an institution with the necessary political clout to directorates headed by senior executives or political appointees and/or reporting to the centre of government (OECD, 2016a). This arrangement has provided the authorities in charge of digital government with the political support to co-ordinate and steer in order to achieve transversal reform and drive government-wide change, to establish agile and collaborative approaches across the administration; and create incentives that support cultural change. This set-up also ensures adequate levels of resources, accountability, specialisation and a reasonable scope for organisational performance assessment. Just as importantly, these digitalisation agencies have been endowed with the budget, convening and enforcement power required to accelerate the development of a robust and dynamic digital ecosystem, allowing for sustained and effective efforts in government transformation.

Organisational frameworks to deliver on digital ambitions

Since 2001, Mexico has progressively taken steps to improve the organisational structures supporting its public sector digitalisation and modernisation efforts. The partnership between the Coordination of the National Digital Strategy and the Ministry of Public Administration has allowed the government of Mexico to achieve more robust integration of digital efforts, from connectivity to the digital economy and society as well as government transformation. It has also secured enough political capital to launch an ambitious, mission-driven initiative to overhaul the government services portal.

Stronger digital government co-ordination has been favoured by the National Digital Strategy and its Coordination office; an increasingly robust legal and regulatory framework; and a set of standards, guidelines and toolkits that have allowed the public administration to progressively harmonise processes and procedures in the federal public administration. Furthermore, the Executive Council Inter-ministerial Commission for e Government Development (Comisión Intersecretarial para el Desarrollo del Gobierno Electrónico, CIDGE) has ensured technical and operational co-ordination of the implementation of the strategy. The sub-commissions and technical teams of the CIDGE have proved to be critical in the operationalisation of key components of the National Digital Strategy.

However, while these mechanisms have brought Mexico a long way in terms of technical co-ordination, their limitations become evident when it comes to high-level political co ordination. The highest ranking co-ordination body for digital government implementation, the CIDGE, meets only at the level of heads of ICT units. While this co ordination structure has been tremendously important so far, it is unclear whether it will be sufficient going forward to secure the political support required to sustain the horizontal and transversal evolution required by the digital transformation.

Given that digital decisions will inevitably become more intertwined with organisation-wide strategic and political decisions, a space or body for high-level political co-ordination and strategic orientation on digital matters becomes increasingly necessary.

Box 1. Proposals for action

Based on the assessment advanced above, Mexico might benefit from considering the following actions:

- Continue to support infrastructure development, access to telecommunications services and Internet connectivity as a means to achieve universal digital inclusion; in particular by identifying key gaps and the actions that would deliver the most impact and progress.
- Double down on the focus of user experience and starting with user needs as the structuring elements of any digital government strategy. This means constantly reviewing policies, regulations, frameworks, standards, guidelines, handbooks and incentives to foster a user-driven culture in the public administration. This would also allow for the emergence of a digital by design approach that supports multi-channel service delivery, contributing to an inclusive government transformation process.
- Further structuring and advancing its efforts for the development of digital skills and inclusion. It would be important in particular to deploy more ambitious pilots and actions to develop digital skills, not only among students and teachers, but across the public sector and all excluded groups, including the elderly, low-income or low-education workers, among others. The authority responsible for the National Digital Strategy could also consider working the Ministry of Public Administration and the Ministry of Labour and Social Welfare to map skills gaps and deploy reskilling and upskilling programmes for civil servants and workers at risk of automation and technological displacement. These programmes should take a broad view on human resources and compensation management to ensure that digital skills and talent are duly recognised. Public sector skills strengthening would benefit from looking at both user skills throughout the public sector and professional skills for IT or digital professionals.
- Empower digital transformation officers within departments, in particular by establishing more direct relationships between the digital leaders or digital transformation officers within institutions and the political leadership of their organisation. These include the introduction of leadership skills and seniority in the competency framework of digital transformation officers, sensitisation programmes on digital transformation for senior political leaders, and other incentives, such as recognitions or awards.
- Build on the accomplishments achieved in the realm of interoperability to achieve end-to-end digital services and seamless government. This initial success exemplified by the InteroperaMX, the interoperable birth certificate and the Single Identity Number for the Population Registry, digital identity and the advanced electronic signature provides the basis for progressive scale. Scaling up these efforts would ease interactions between levels of government. Most importantly, the continuous expansion of the use of these interoperable components would enable the public administration to better serve users, making life easier for citizens. Future efforts might do well by continuing to focus on key national registries to unlock the power of data sharing to simplify service delivery. An area of additional interest that is worth exploring is how to establish a stronger consent model to provide service users with greater control about how their data are used by the public authorities and/or shared, as countries like Belgium, Estonia, the Netherlands and Spain are doing.
- Continue to strengthen the open government data ecosystem through the implementation of the recommendations in the OECD report Open Government Data in Mexico: The Way Forward.
- Establish a high-level collegial body to provide overall political orientation and strategic co-ordination of digital government policy and issues of relevance for the National Digital Strategy. This body would not replace the very much needed implementation co-ordination level that

> brings together the leaders of ICT units across the federal administration, but would be a new level of governance engaging senior organisational leadership.
> - Set up a governance and organisational arrangements that support the effective and sustained implementation of the National Digital Strategy. These arrangements should grant the authority responsible for overseeing the implementation of the strategy with an adequate mandate, securing the necessary level of authority and political influence. These organisational arrangements should also provide levels of accountability that offer incentives to take action. Setting up an agency for digital transformation attached to an institution with the necessary political clout (e.g. the Office of the President or the Ministry of Finance), while securing the agency's leadership, could provide the right framework for sustainable success. This path could ensure the influence to steer changes across sectors, while isolating the agency from the risk of changing executives within those ministries that may or may not be as interested in the digitalisation agenda.

Strides towards a digital and user-driven administration in Mexico

Digital service transformation starts with user needs

Mexico has joined other trend-setter OECD countries in developing design principles, standards, guides and other requirements for digital public service delivery. This trend has given rise to the internationally recognised Principles for Digital Development[1] and the OECD's forthcoming General Digital Service Design Principles. These powerful tools have encouraged digital teams across the administration not to simply digitalise paper-based procedures, but to focus on digitalisation efforts to redesign processes.

By providing digital teams with a principle-based approach to service design, these tools empower them to leave behind obsolete rules and refocus efforts on user-driven approaches. These tools are of critical importance for the successful transformation of service delivery. All digital service delivery strategies start with user needs and these tools help governments to refocus its attention and efforts on understanding those needs. These tools have also provided a clear definition of what performing services are. The power of such standards and principles has been magnified by the governance framework put around the government's single portal Gob.mx, which have allowed the Digital Government Unit to be able to determine whether a digital service complies with the standards and is good enough to go on the portal, thus serving as quality control. Along with the government's Seal of Excellence, a government tool providing incentives for compliance with government guidelines and standards, the framework for digital services has brought Mexico a long way.

However, a push from the centre can only go so far and is unlikely to deliver lasting, government-wide cultural transformation across the administration and levels of government. One answer for this dilemma is embedding digital leadership and approaches across departments and levels of government. It is important to understand that digital leaders are not IT specialists, but individuals who can strategically leverage the power and principles of technologies to achieve the organisations' strategic objectives. In this sense, the position of digital transformation officer must go beyond a fancy title to overcome the biased perception of them being perceived as an IT support system. To help drive change, digital transformation officers must be politically able, and stay close to the ears of organisational boards and become the voice of service users within the organisation.

Furthermore, as digital governments achieve new levels of maturity, they have been looking for ways to improve their own digital service standards. The United Kingdom, an OECD peer and trend-setter in this domain, is the clearest example. The Government Digital Service is working on a revised framework that will focus, among others, on fostering more joined up approaches rather than simply transforming individual services (Gill, 12 September 2018). This means a greater focus on what the user is ultimately trying to achieve rather than departmental individual mandates or responsibilities. Mexico would also benefit from a greater focus on the user journey and life events in the mid- to long term as a means to achieving more substantial, user-driven transformation.

Finally, Mexico has a significant number of citizens residing abroad (12 million). Digital service transformation could also yield benefits by better serving Mexicans, foreign investors and other user groups abroad, bringing government closer to these constituents.

A data culture that supports the delivery of policy outcomes and social change

The government of Mexico has embedded the relevance of data for the digital transformation in the National Digital Strategy (Government of Mexico, 2013), and has made concrete efforts to build the institutional, social and economic infrastructure around it to support it (OECD, 2016b; 2018b). Furthermore, it has progressively built the necessary institutional capabilities and the organisational underpinnings to achieve increasing levels of sophistication in the use of data in the public sector to address priority policy issues. Efforts such as the institutionalisation of chief data officers and digital transformation officers are of remarkable importance to advancing the data operations of the public sector (OECD, 2018b).

Mexico has also maintained a healthy interest in disruptive emerging data-processing technologies that will upend industries, such as artificial intelligence (AI). Indeed, the government of Mexico is expected to show leadership in this area of critical importance for its sustained economic development. The Coordination of the National Digital Strategy worked with the British Embassy in Mexico, Oxford Insights and C Minds to develop a roadmap for the effective and ethical AI in the country (Dutton, 2018; Martinho Truswell et al., 2018; Zapata, 22 March 2018). In addition, the government of Mexico has supported the creation of ia2030, a multi-sectoral partnership to set the course for AI development in the country. This is consistent with trends across OECD countries as highlighted by the work of the OECD E-Leaders' Thematic Group on Emerging Technologies. Mexico has largely succeeded in making the case for the relevance of data-driven approaches going forward. The question today is how to nurture a data-driven culture in the public sector that is ingrained in public sector operations, strategic priorities and policy objectives.

One first objective might be ensuring that public organisations are able to look beyond the hype and have a thorough understanding of technologies' opportunities, but also understanding their limitations and what they cannot achieve. A clear-eyed view that understands that data can be a critical strategic asset to improve the public sector's strategic foresight, public service delivery and performance monitoring, and deploys data capabilities consequently. Data science skills are scarce. The initiative Retos Publicos, later renamed Retos MX, responded to the need to foster the capacity of the Mexican public sector to let policy issues and strategic questions drive efforts aimed to foster data-driven approaches (Díaz, Rowshankish and Saleh, 2018). Additionally, data analytics have been successfully deployed in digital service delivery through the Gob.mx portal, but cases of successful implementation for policy making are still rare. The data governance in the Mexican federal public administration should be reinforced to keep encouraging and expanding the implementation of data-driven techniques in highly strategic ways through frameworks, incentives, guidance and capacity building.

While frameworks and systems are critical, culture ultimately relies on people and is preserved by senior leadership. The speed and depth of technological change exposes political leaders to great risk of failure if they do not understand the strategic implications of these changes and of the choices in front of them (Díaz, Rowshankish and Saleh, 2018). This might suggest the need for more direct linkages and effective co ordination and lines of communications between chief data officers and digital transformation officers and the top decision makers in the organisation. As top-level decision makers progressively see how technology and data can make them more effective executives, this relationship is bound to gain the digital and data-driven culture support.

Ultimately, to embed a data-driven culture into the fabric of the state, regardless of changing administrations, chief data officers and data scientists must be able to effectively work with business units and operations. By making the latter improve the delivery of their respective functions, thus enhancing organisational performance, chief data officers and their teams will gain growing support, interest and demand from the different parts of the organisation.

The Mexican public sector would also benefit from focusing early data-driven missions to improve public sector performance in areas that require substantial effort and resources, thus ensuring high returns on investment. For instance, predictive maintenance of infrastructure and equipment could lead to substantial savings of resources and lives (Bender, Henke and Lamarre, 2018).

Building digital capability in the Mexican public sector

Government transformation is first and foremost about transforming the way government works and building new capabilities and a culture that supports delivery. Digitalisation will transform the future of work, requiring new skills in every sector and industry (Chui, Manyika and Miremadi, 2015; Manyika et al., 2017), including governments. Decades of outsourcing IT delivery and maintenance in government has probably undermined the public sector's ability to manage and deliver IT projects, not to mention digital design and delivery approaches. The Mexican public sector faces the need to deploy strategies to reskill, upskill and acquire new talent in order to deliver on its digital ambitions.

To tackle this issue, the government of Mexico launched its new Digital Academy,[2] a platform providing civil servants access to online courses. It also provides guidance on how to obtain access to in-person digital government training workshops organised by the Digital Government Unit of the Ministry of Public Administration. While this is an important first step in upskilling civil servants, these activities do not yet have the scope or scale needed to respond to the challenge of the digital transformation.

It is important for the Mexican public sector to clearly differentiate between the skills that it may need to acquire and the capabilities it can build internally by reskilling and retraining existing staff. Project managers and other roles can be retrained to identify digital opportunities and use agile or DevOps methodologies instead of waterfall project management relatively easy. However, areas like data science, machine learning, artificial intelligence or even human-centred design require very specific skills, backgrounds and experience which are hard to transfer (Bughin et al., 2018). In addition, talent in these areas is scarce and in high demand, but very much needed for a successful digital transformation.

Mexico might benefit from mapping the existing skills gap within the public sector as a basis to develop a strategy to quickly attract new digital talent to the public sector, while these new skills become more available and are able to spread more broadly across the public sector. For this, the government of Mexico would have to map skill needs with the government's priorities and choose better candidates in addition to making public sector employment or missions more attractive for these highly skilled individuals, by creating appropriate job profiles.

Ensuring that the hiring process is more agile and candidates are tested for relevant abilities and skills is part of the redesigning process of public employment in support of the digital transformation, e.g. recruiting staff to build a data-driven skilled administration implies testing candidates capable of data mining, processing massive amounts of data or setting up data collection techniques for a given service (Bracken and Greenway, 2018; Bracken et al., 2018) through a panel bringing together multidisciplinary profiles with expertise that can provide a robust assessment of the actual knowledge and capabilities of the candidate.

In addition, roles should be clearly defined and titles should not be used loosely. If public organisations call any data analysis role a data scientist, the clarity, value and prestige that comes with the title will erode, making it harder to attract talent from the private sector. Clarifying roles, responsibilities and expectations around them could be a beneficial development. This suggests the relevance of efforts targeted towards the development of competency frameworks as key for digital and data-related positions in the public sector as well as the importance of clarifying their role and responsibilities.

ICT acquisition frameworks to support more integrated and agile delivery are another area of potential improvement. Through the ICT Policy,[3] its implementation guides and handbooks,[4] the government of Mexico has established a clear process for conducting an ICT commissioning exercise and structuring ICT projects. These include basic requirements, such as the use of open standards, reusable components, digital identity and meeting interoperability requirements. In addition, the current policy is sound in identifying the team, establishing ICT project catalogues, performing feasibility studies, structuring a business case and providing clear definitions of minimum requirements. These specifications are made more robust by the use of the digital government Seal of Excellence,[5] granted to those services that meet the existing digital government standards and which have gone through a robust process of development.

The government of Mexico has also set up framework agreements for software licensing with 31 software providers,[6] which has the value of making procurement simpler and more agile. Moreover, the government is currently developing a software framework agreement to efficiently respond to the software needs of public organisations.[7] While these efforts are greatly valuable as they save the public sector time and resources, more can be done to adjust the procurement process in order to expand the number of providers participating in this sort of agreement, to limit concentration, to make access to business opportunities more inclusive and to expand the pool of providers to the state. Ultimately, 31 firms are just too few to ensure adequate competition among providers and licensing agreements are not enough to respond to the need of more tailored solutions.

Procurement frameworks and business cases would also benefit from clarifying the approach and contracting modalities to facilitate the use of agile methodologies. The ICT Policy asks project managers to define service requirements and functionalities in advance. This is sensible, but recognition is needed for the fact that new functionalities and requirements may and will be revealed in the testing or roll-out stages, requiring further iteration and improvement. While the digital standard and the service design principles of the government of Mexico provide guidance to project managers on how to manage digitalisation initiatives, the ICT Policy and handbook do not clearly advise on how to conduct the procurement process or structure contracts to effectively use agile approaches.

If not carefully structured, contracts may require successive extensions to address problems with the solutions delivered, improve functionality or user experience, which may be uneconomical and inefficient. Moreover, IT project management frameworks and guidance might benefit from encouraging practitioners to adopt more joined-up management approaches.

Box 2. Proposals for action

Based on the assessment advanced above, Mexico might benefit from considering the following actions:

- Digital strategies start with user needs. Reassess standards, design principles, guidelines and other tools to take them to their next level of maturity, fostering more proactive delivery of services around users' needs and goals (e.g. linked to life events) that needs to rely on joined up approaches to service delivery. Understanding users' needs allows the public administration to take a digital-by-design approach that supports multi-channel service delivery, promoting a government transformation that is inclusive in a country that still faces significant digital, social and economic divides.

- Explore opportunities in cross-border services to better serve Mexican citizens abroad, foreign investors and other users. In particular, the promotion of cross border services in North America, Europe and Latin America could yield important economic and social benefits for the country.

- Make efforts to grow digital leadership across departments. In particular, identify criteria to select and assign digital transformation officers across ministries with adequate leadership skills, powers and access to the political leadership to be able to underline the importance of digital transformation for the government in different sectors. Nurture communities of practices within government in key areas, such as service design, user research and digital delivery.

- Define and adopt a formalised strategic approach to govern the management of the whole value chain of government data in alignment with the recommendations advanced in the OECD report Open Government Data in Mexico: The Way Forward. This action should include: the deployment of data driven efforts strategically to tackle clearly defined policy or operational problems (e.g. to link prioritisation of data release in open formats with broader policy objectives or policy issues); the development of capabilities for data use driven by a problem solving approach to create value and nurture political support; consider high-impact interventions, such as predictive infrastructure maintenance.

- Demonstrate the value of data for the core business of different public sector organisations, working with them to identify priority data sets to improve their performance and operations. These efforts should acknowledge the contribution of the business units and operations across the public sector to guide decisions on data (e.g. for increased sharing, interoperability, opening up) led by the demand of users across the public sector. This would secure efforts that can be scaled up and improve public sector performance as rooted in the core business of government. Ultimately, working together with business units on data-driven approaches will help organisations more clearly define what to do, understand how to do it and assess the success of interventions.

- Develop a strategy for acquiring new talent in critical areas and upskilling the existing public sector workforce. In particular, take measures to rapidly build data science, service design and human-centred design capabilities across the public sector. In addition, deploy a structured upskilling programme for civil servants, training them in essential skills for managers, such as agile procurement, management and development.

- Clarify digital, data, and ICT roles and competency frameworks in the public sector. In doing this, Mexico might benefit from clearly defining key roles to increase its maturity as a digital government, including digital transformation officer, product and delivery managers, user researchers, data scientist, data analysts, data engineer, data architect. Providing clarity of roles and assigned responsibilities; aligning human resources management, compensation and recognition policies; and building a culture that provides the correct incentives and space for

> these new roles to properly exert their role would be essential. The federal public administration would thus be better able to protect the status of these roles and their ability to influence change.
> - Review talent acquisition frameworks to provide fit-for-purpose environments for hiring highly technical talent. These adjustments could seek to ensure contracting procedures that are clear and agile and that test the core skills of the mission.
> - Review business cases and ICT commissioning frameworks so they are in line with digital service standards and principles and that they enable the administration to focus on delivery and outcomes. These investment frameworks would ideally allow the public sector to roll out agile contracting approaches and joined-up digital delivery models (such as DevOps) instead of waterfall project management. These approaches would also benefit from testing proof of concept and providers' capability to deliver first, instead of during the implementation phase. Achieving this may require the revisiting of project funding and spending control frameworks.
> - Increase the variety of providers with framework agreements that encourage competition and diversity in ICT providers for the public sector. The software framework agreement currently being developed would also benefit from clearly stating the expectation of use of agile, iterative approaches laid out in the digital standards and service design principles of the Mexican public sector. These policy measures would enable the federal administration to open up to a number of newly emerging service providers in the digital age (e.g. start-ups, social entrepreneurs), thus bringing more efficiency to the public sector while contributing to the economic growth of new actors in emerging sectors.

References

Bender, M., N. Henke and E. Lamarre (2018), "The cornerstones of large-scale technology transformation", McKinsey Quarterly, October, https://www.mckinsey.com/business-functions/digital-mckinsey/our-insights/the-cornerstones-of-large-scale-technology-transformation.

Bracken, M. and Greenway, A. (2018), How to Achieve and Sustain Government Digital Transformation, Inter-American Development Bank, Washington, DC, http://dx.doi.org/10.18235/0001215.

Bracken, M. et al. (2018), Digital Transformation at Scale: Why the Strategy is Delivery, London Publishing Partnership, London.

Bughin, J. et al. (2018), "Why digital strategies fail", McKinsey Quarterly, January, https://www.mckinsey.com/business-functions/digital-mckinsey/our-insights/why-digital-strategies-fail.

Chui, M., J. Manyika and M. Miremadi (2015), "Four fundamentals of workplace automation", McKinsey Quarterly, November, https://www.mckinsey.com/business-functions/digital-mckinsey/our-insights/four-fundamentals-of-workplace-automation.

Díaz, A., K. Rowshankish and T. Saleh (2018), "Why data culture matters", McKinsey Quarterly, September, https://www.mckinsey.com/business-functions/mckinsey-analytics/our-insights/why-data-culture-matters.

Dutton, T. (2018), "Artificial intelligence strategies", Medium.com - Politics + AI.

Gill, S. (12 September 2018), "What's happening with the service standard?", Government Digital Service blog, https://gds.blog.gov.uk/2018/09/12/whats-happening-with-the-service-standard.

Government of Mexico (2013), Estrategia Digital Nacional, Presidencia de los Estados Unidos Mexicanos.

IDB (2018), Wait No More: Citizens, Red Tape and Digital Government, Roseth, B., a. Reyes and C. Santiso (eds.), Inter-American Develpoment Bank, Washington, DC, https://publications.iadb.org/handle/11319/8930.

Manyika, J. et al. (2017), "Jobs lost, jobs gained: What the future of work will mean for jobs, skills, and wages", McKinsey Global Institute, https://www.mckinsey.com/~/media/McKinsey/Featured%20Insights/Future%20of%20Organizations/What%20the%20future%20of%20work%20will%20mean%20for%20jobs%20skills%20and%20wages/MGI-Jobs-Lost-Jobs-Gained-Report-December-6-2017.ashx.

Martinho-Truswell, E. et al. (2018), "Towards an AI strategy in Mexico: Harnessing the AI revolution", White Paper, British Embassy Mexico City, Oxford Insights and C Minds.

OECD (2019), "The digital transformation of the public sector: Helping governments respond to the needs of networked societies", OECD, Paris, forthcoming.

OECD (2018a), "Digital Government Survey 2018", OECD, Paris.

OECD (2018b), Open Government Data in Mexico: The Way Forward, OECD Publishing, Paris, https://doi.org/10.1787/9789264297944-en.

OECD (2018c), Open Government Data Report: Enhancing Policy Maturity for Sustainable Impact, OECD Digital Government Studies, OECD Publishing, Paris, http://dx.doi.org/10.1787/9789264305847-en.

OECD (2016a), Digital Government in Chile, OECD Publishing, Paris, https://doi.org/10.1787/9789264258013-en.

OECD (2016b), Open Government Data Review of Mexico: Data Reuse for Public Sector Impact and Innovation, OECD Publishing, Paris, https://doi.org/10.1787/9789264259270-en.

OECD (2014), "Recommendation of the Council on Digital Government Strategies", OECD, Paris, https://www.oecd.org/gov/digital-government/Recommendation-digital-government-strategies.pdf.

Ubaldi, B. (2013), "Open government data: Towards empirical analysis of open government data initiatives", OECD Working Papers on Public Governance, No. 22, OECD Publishing, Paris, http://dx.doi.org/10.1787/5k46bj4f03s7-en.

Zapata, E. (22 March 2018), "Estrategia de inteligencia artificial MX 2018, Gob.mx", México Digital Blog, https://www.gob.mx/mexicodigital/articulos/estrategia-de-inteligencia-artificial-mx-2018.

Notes

[1] https://digitalprinciples.org.

[2] https://www.gob.mx/academiadigital.

[3] https://www.gob.mx/cms/uploads/attachment/file/380408/MAAGTICSI_compilado__20182208.pdf.

[4] https://www.gob.mx/cms/uploads/attachment/file/32502/Guia-CUTIC.pdf.

[5] www.dof.gob.mx/nota_detalle.php?codigo=5446678&fecha=03/08/2016.

[6] https://www.gob.mx/sfp/documentos/contrato-marco-licencias-de-software.

[7] https://www.gob.mx/sfp/documentos/contrato-marco-software?state=published.

1 The case for a digital government in Mexico

This chapter discusses the technological trends and the new policy scenario brought about by the 4th industrial revolution. Growing connectivity and new emerging technologies such as the Internet of Things, blockchain, cloud computing, data analytics and artificial intelligence enable new production and delivery models. These new business models allow for greater organisational performance, improved decision-making and services that better respond to user needs. The chapter analyses what these changes mean for the Mexican public sector, and why governments have put digital government at the core of public sector reform. The chapter advances a framework for understanding digital government and explains how it can help the government of Mexico achieve its policy objectives.

The age of disruption

The world is facing an age of dramatic technological change. The speed, depth and breadth of change promises to reshape economies and societies across the globe. Financial services in rural areas are being delivered through mobile phones, distributed networks and blockchain-based solutions challenge existing business models, self-driving cars are taking the streets, artificial intelligence (AI) prepares to transform medical science, and the Internet of Things (IoT) has opened the road for the rise of digital cities. Data have become a critical strategic resource, so much so that it has been famously referred to as the oil of the 21st century (The Economist, 2017).

Still, the digital revolution is in its early stages and more rapid innovation should be expected as our ability to produce, store and process massive amounts of data accelerates. To put things into perspective and assess the significance of these changes, and the potential for societal transformation, one has but to think that in 1995, barely 4% of the world population was on line (OECD, 2017a). Even today, only 48% of the world population use the Internet (International Telecommunications Union, 2017). The OECD estimates that as digital technologies such as IoT, AI, machine learning, robotics and 3D printing become more ubiquitous and combined with new biotechnologies, the world will see a new production revolution of a scope and speed that have never been seen before (OECD, 2017b).

Klaus Schwab, Founder and Executive Chairman of the World Economic Forum, has convincingly argued that we are entering the fourth industrial revolution (Schwab, 2016). He suggests that current technological trends will significantly transform the production models of goods and services, patterns in socialisation as well as the way governments operate and interact with their constituents. According to Schwab, the fourth industrial revolution will be unique in its speed, scope and complexity, and will be characterised by exponential productivity growth.

Indeed, today's most valuable companies are those that are able to harness the power of technology and data to gain deeper insights, build closer relationships with their customers, and re-engineer their production processes and service offerings. As markets closed at the end of September 2018, seven of the ten most valuable companies in the world were technology companies. The OECD has found that the ability to use technology and data strategically is a significant factor in explaining the growing productivity gap among firms (Andrews, Criscuolo and Gal, 2015; 2016).

In addition, the world, and OECD countries in particular, has seen the rise of the first generation of digital natives; that is, individuals that grew up connected to the Internet through digital devices. A generation that learns, socialises, works and accesses services in a radically different way than any generation that came before it. A generation that requires very different administrative arrangements and a new digital social contract. For instance, the digital natives will require a very different set of skills to succeed in the digital era than the generation of their parents (or any other before it).

As the pace of change accelerates, governments around the world must not only be able to keep abreast of technological changes as regulators, but they should also be equipped with a broader understanding of how new technologies are changing expectations about public services and policies and the capabilities to act on them. For too long governments from around the world have outsourced digital skills and capability, which has progressively eroded their ability to respond to the rapid technological changes of the fourth industrial revolution. Public authorities have realised that they have some catching up to do in order to update governance arrangements and transform business processes to meet the challenges of the 21st century. Analogue governments cannot effectively serve digital economies and societies.

The government of Mexico has strived to keep up with the pace of change. As its start-up ecosystem matures, the Latin American country has sought to create a conducive environment that allows technology-driven innovation to thrive. Most recently, the approval of the new FinTech law, in force since September 2018, set up a framework for structuring and publicly sharing application programming interfaces in the financial industry to support open digital innovation (OECD, 2018). The law stands as the clear acknowledgement of Mexico's willingness of the need of keep up with the rapid digitalisation of the economy.

Mexico has also made significant efforts to modernise public sector operations, striving to achieve fully mature digital government implementation. Still, 27% of government transactions in the country require three or more interactions and users of public services in Mexico need an average of 6.9 hours to complete a transaction (IDB, 2018), above the average for the region (25% and 5.4 hours respectively).

The question going forward is not if, but how, to digitalise government and how to do it in a sufficiently agile and sustainable manner to keep serving businesses and citizens ever more effectively. The question has significant import. McKinsey, a consultancy firm, estimates that governments will be spending over USD 1 trillion annually worldwide by 2025 to digitalise their services, with potential cost savings of 60-75% on administrative task (Manyika et al., 2013). The government of Mexico alone had mapped 120 public sector ICT projects with budgets above USD 10 million in 2014 (OECD, 2015). However, the benefits of these massive investments in digitalisation will only be realised if they are guided by a strategic approach that is supported by the right governance frameworks, business processes, culture and capability (OECD, 2014). This realisation has put digital transformation at the centre of public sector reform agendas around the world.

Digital government at the core of public sector reform

The fast-paced development of the digital ecosystems in which public sectors operate today has brought about new opportunities and new challenges for governments. Access to mobile phones has become virtually universal. There are today 104.5 mobile subscriptions per 100 people globally and 78.7% of the OECD population uses the Internet (World Bank, 2018). Mexico itself has seen a profound transformation. The share of Mexicans using the Internet went from 5.1% in 2000 to 31.1% in 2010 and 63.9% in 2017 (World Bank, 2018). Mobile phone penetration has experienced even faster growth (even if it has stalled in recent years), from 13.9 subscriptions per 100 people in 2000 to 77.9 in 2010 and 88.5 in 2017 (World Bank, 2018).

Unprecedented levels of home-based and mobile connectivity make it possible to deliver public services in ways that are more convenient and that generate data to enable continuous improvement, while saving time and resources for users and the public sector. Yet, despite continuous progress in the adoption and use of digital technologies, the digital divide and digital exclusion remain as significant challenges to be tackled (OECD, 2017e).

Beginning in the late 1990s, governments set out to implement e-government – "the use of information and communication technologies (ICTs), and particularly the Internet, to achieve better government" (OECD, 2014). These initiatives aimed at responding to the growing demand for more responsive, efficient, effective and participatory government. National e-government projects succeeded in making public information more readily available and putting public services on line as a means of modernisation. These reforms had important achievements, allowing in effect individuals and businesses to more conveniently access services remotely and public administrations to achieve efficiency gains in service delivery.

While the OECD was early in calling for a whole-of-government approach, common business processes and greater integration (OECD, 2003, 2005, 2009), the e-government wave had a number shortcomings. Most notably, it left a legacy of siloed systems, digital fragmentation and the digitisation of systems without significant transformation – from processes to organisational culture. The digital maturity of public sector organisations, but most importantly, its leadership, governance frameworks and the digital capability of the public sector, were not conducive to the emergence of modern, digital governments.

Mexico was not the exception to this trend. The push for digitalisation coming from the centre, driven by the Coordination of the National Digital Strategy at the Office of the President, has achieved significant success. Today roughly 90% of government transactions can be initiated on line and 75% can be completed digitally (IDB, 2018), making Mexico the uncontested leader in the region by this metric[1]. Nevertheless, only 10% of Mexicans reported completing their last government transaction through digital channels and several interactions with government are too often needed to complete a single transaction (IDB, 2018). This suggests that Mexico has yet to reap the full benefits of digital government in terms of enhancing interactions with government by enabling a multi-channel, joined-up and user-driven approach.

This conclusion is in tune with the paradigm shift in the use of technology in the public sector. This shift has been driven by growing fiscal pressures, citizens' expectations of greater openness, the limitations of siloed systems and a more dynamic environment of digital innovation. There is growing awareness among relevant stakeholders of the critical role digital technologies can play in ensuring public sector effectiveness, helping achieve critical policy objectives such as sustainable development, public trust and overall public sector performance. This paradigm shift is embodied by the transition from e-government to digital government, characterised by dramatic change in how the public administration relates with citizens and businesses.

Digital government uses technology to enable open, user-driven, proactive and inclusive public services; redesign government processes; and take data-driven decisions. The strategic use of technologies in the public sector also enables the rise of government as a platform and facilitates greater integration of services, but also deeper collaboration and sharing within and outside of the public sector, from innovative ICT commissioning processes to open government data and crowdsourcing of collective knowledge (OECD, forthcoming). Digital government is about users taking the centre stage by putting digital technologies and data as strategic tools at the core of the public sector reform agenda (OECD, 2014).

To keep in tune with this age of disruption, OECD governments, including Mexico, must be able to integrate digital tools and approaches into their DNA, or else be increasingly challenged by new business models and players that are better able to meet the needs of citizens and businesses. Not adapting, failing to deliver the quality services citizens expect and policy failures due to the lack of technological capability could mean a rapid erosion of trust in public institutions. Public organisations would thus be challenged by new digital organisations and become less relevant and capable. Ultimately, they might lose the standing and strategic position to help set up their national economies for success in the 21st century.

The OECD has identified six areas of intervention that can help to restore, sustain or increase levels of trust in government (OECD, 2017c; 2017d):

1. **Reliability**: Governments have an obligation to minimise uncertainty in the economic, social and political environment.
2. **Responsiveness**: Trust in government can depend on a citizen's experience when receiving public services – a crucial factor of trust in government.
3. **Openness**: Open government policies that concentrate on citizen engagement and access to information can increase public trust.
4. **Better regulation**: Proper regulation is important for justice, fairness and the rule of law as well as in delivering public services.
5. **Integrity and fairness**: Integrity is a crucial determinant of trust and is essential if governments want to be recognised as clean, fair and open.
6. **Inclusive policy making**: Understanding how policies are designed can strengthen institutions and promote trust between government and citizens.

Figure 1.1. The digital transformation of the public sector

Digital transformation of the public sector

Analogue government
- Analogue procedures.
- Closed operations and internal focus.
- Government as a provider.

E-government
- ICT-enabled procedures, but often analogue in design.
- User-centred approach, but supply driven. One-way communications and service delivery.
- Siloed ICT development and acquisition.
- Government as a provider.

Digital government
- Procedures that are digital by design.
- User-driven public administration.
- Government as a platform (co-creation).
- Open by default (co-creation).
- Data-driven public sector.
- Proactive administration.

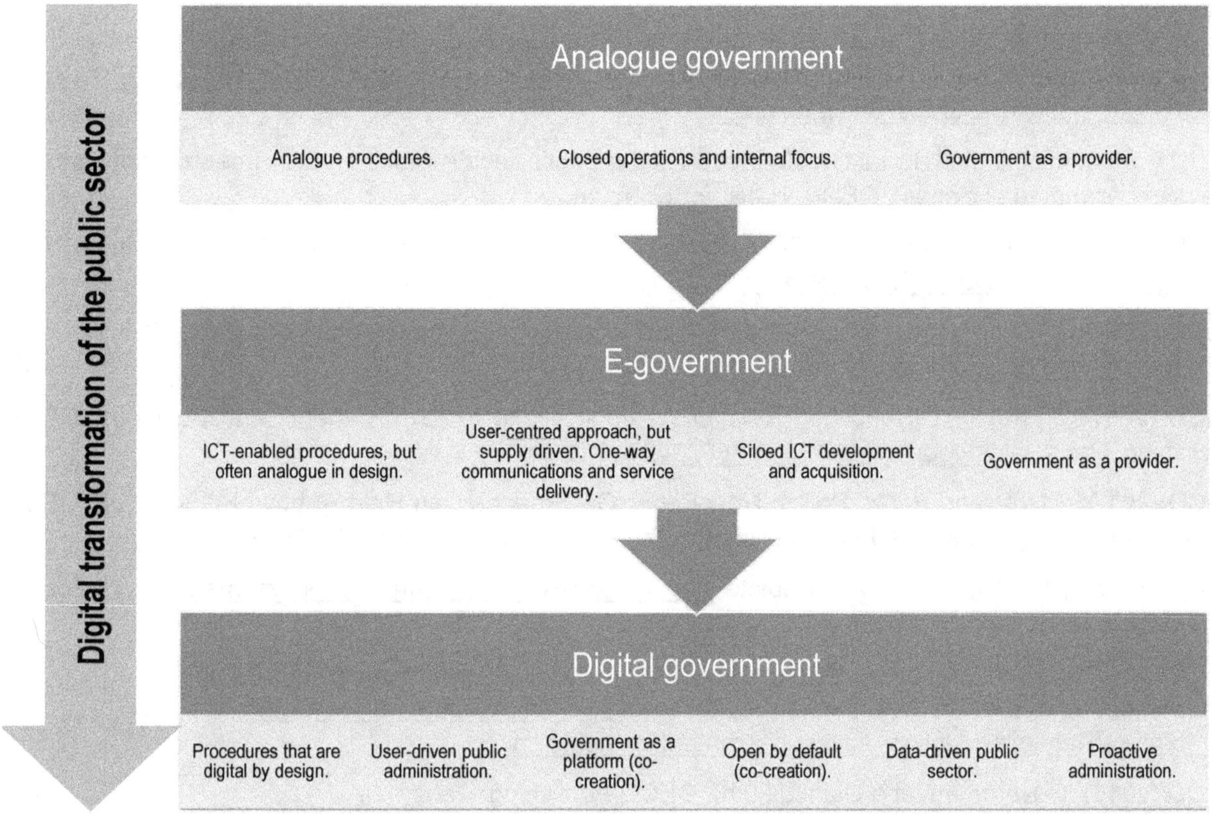

Source: OECD (forthcoming), "The digital transformation of the public sector: Helping governments respond to the needs of networked societies".

Digital government significantly advances state capability to deliver results across these dimensions by making government more data- and evidence-driven, enabling it to act as a platform that leverages collective intelligence by facilitating co-creation with internal and external stakeholders, and strengthening transparency and accountability. All of these characteristics result in more robust, user-driven, proactive and effective policy making, and service delivery arrangements and solutions. Digital government has become an essential policy area, not so much for the future of government, but for its present and continuous modernisation efforts.

References

Andrews, D., C. Criscuolo and P. Gal (2016), "The best versus the rest: The global productivity slowdown, divergence across firms and the role of public policy", OECD Productivity Working Papers, No. 5, OECD Publishing, Paris, https://doi.org/10.1787/63629cc9-en.

Andrews, D., C. Criscuolo and P. Gal (2015), "Frontier firms, technology diffusion and public policy: Micro evidence from OECD countries", OECD Productivity Working Papers, No. 2, OECD Publishing, Paris, https://doi.org/10.1787/5jrql2q2jj7b-en.

IDB (2018), Wait No More: Citizens, Red Tape and Digital Government, Roseth, B., a. Reyes and C. Santiso (eds.), Inter-American Develpoment Bank, Washington, DC, https://publications.iadb.org/handle/11319/8930.

International Telecommunication Union (2017), Measuring the Information Society Report 2017, International Telecommunication Union, Geneva.

Manyika, J. et al. (2013), 'Disruptive technologies: Advances that will transform life business, and the global economy', McKinsey Global Institute, May. https://www.mckinsey.com/business-functions/digital-mckinsey/our-insights/disruptive-technologies.

OECD (forthcoming), "The digital transformation of the public sector: Helping governments respond to the needs of networked societies", OECD, Paris, forthcoming.

OECD (2018), Open Government Data in Mexico: The Way Forward, OECD Publishing, Paris, https://doi.org/10.1787/9789264297944-en.

OECD (2017a), "Going digital: Making the transformation work for growth and well being", OECD, Paris, https://www.oecd.org/mcm/documents/C-MIN-2017-4%20EN.pdf.

OECD (2017b), The Next Production Revolution: Implications for Governments and Business, OECD Publishing, Paris, https://doi.org/10.1787/9789264271036-en.

OECD (2017c), Trust and Public Policy: How Better Governance Can Help Rebuild Public Trust, OECD Public Governance Reviews, OECD Publishing, Paris, https://doi.org/10.1787/9789264268920-en.

OECD (2017d), Trust in government website, http://www.oecd.org/gov/trust-in-government.htm (accessed 13 March 2019).

OECD (2017e), "Report on the implementation of the Recommendation of the Council on Digital Government Strategies", C(2017)139, OECD, Paris, https://www.oecd.org/gov/digital-government/Recommendation-digital-government-strategies.pdf.

OECD (2015), Government at a Glance 2015, OECD Publishing, Paris, https://doi.org/10.1787/gov_glance-2015-en.

OECD (2014), "Recommendation of the Council on Digital Government Strategies", OECD, Paris, https://www.oecd.org/gov/digital-government/Recommendation-digital-government-strategies.pdf.

OECD (2009), Rethinking e-Government Services: User-Centred Approaches, OECD e Government Series, OECD Publishing, Paris, https://doi.org/10.1787/9789264059412-en.

OECD (2005), e-Government for Better Government, OECD e-Government Series, OECD Publishing, Paris, https://doi.org/10.1787/9789264018341-en.

OECD (2003), The e-Government Imperative, OECD e-Government Series, OECD Publishing, Paris, https://doi.org/10.1787/9789264101197-en.

Schwab, K. (2016), The Fourth Industrial Revolution, World Economic Forum. Geneva.

The Economist (2017), "Data is giving rise to a new economy", The Economist, 6 May.

World Bank (2018), World Development Indicators (database), World Bank, Washington, DC, https://datacatalog.worldbank.org/dataset/world-development-indicators.

Note

[1] While in Uruguay 100% of government transactions can be initiated digitally, only 40% of them can be completed digitally from end-to-end.

2 The evolution from e-government to digital government in Mexico

This chapter provides an overview of Mexico's e-government efforts and its collaboration with the OECD to strengthen the use of information and communication technologies to deliver better government. The chapter goes over the main findings and policy recommendations on e-government advanced by the OECD to Mexico in the 2005 OECD e-Government Review of Mexico and the 2011 Public Governance Review of Mexico. Based on those assessments, the chapter identifies pervasive challenges the country has faced in using technology effectively to improve public sector performance and deliver better public services.

Mexico was early to recognise the value of technology in helping reform the public sector and has since been making efforts to achieve excellence. In 2005, the Mexican Ministry of Public Administration (SFP) requested the OECD's support in the form of an OECD e Government Review. The review advanced an assessment of e-government policies, their context, implementation, leadership and organisational challenges, as well as user focus in service delivery and monitoring and evaluation practices. This helped identify both outstanding challenges and opportunities that resulted in the formulation of policy recommendations.

While Mexico had been extensively using ICTs in government since the late 1990s, it wasn't until 2001 that the government of Mexico, through the, now extinct, President's Office for Government Innovation, launched a comprehensive e-government public policy seeking to modernise the Mexican government (OECD, 2005). The new e-government policy became a central element of public sector reform as it became one of the six pillars of the Presidential Agenda for Good Government in late 2002 (OECD, 2005). At the time, the OECD 2005 e-Government Study of Mexico highlighted some notable achievements:

- from 2001 to 2004 the number of services available on line went up from 170 to 922, a 442% increase
- the launch of a single government portal that was internationally recognised as a good practice
- back office improvements in specific areas, such as pensions, taxes, permits, inquiries, public procurement and business services.

Despite these achievements, significant barriers and challenges were identified, including:

- Budgetary barriers: Inflexible budgetary arrangements, uncertain future funds and limited funding did not allow for effective resource sharing, sustainable investments or adequate planning frameworks for e-government projects.
- Regulatory barriers: Complex regulations, lack of recognition of e-government processes and lack of regulatory flexibility were found to be the most important regulatory barriers for e-government development.
- Digital divide: The digital divide significantly hindered the impact and relevance of e-government. Indeed, the share of Mexicans who had access to the Internet in 2001 was a bare 7% and by 2004, two years after the launch of E-Mexico, Mexico's connectivity policy, despite doubling access in just two years, still only 14.1% of the population was using the Internet, significantly lower than the OECD average of 50.5% by 2004 (World Bank, 2018).
- Insufficient institutionalisation: E-government efforts were mostly driven top down, under the leadership of the President's Office for Government Innovation. However, the strategic value of e-government wasn't clearly recognised across all ministries and institutions, nor its potential for supporting other objectives of the Good Government Agenda.
- Need of new skillsets: Public institutions were facing the growing need of new competencies well beyond management. In particular, skills for re engineering processes was a particular area of focus, in particular as many senior managers still viewed e-government as a tool to digitalise and automate existing business processes.
- Low levels of collaboration among agencies: Furthermore, the review found that collaboration among ministries and public institutions was at its infancy, leading to duplication of initiatives, services, registries and systems, in addition to significant fragmentation and lack of interoperability.
- Transparency and service delivery: While some efforts had been carried out to make information more readily available, the review found that not enough had been done to tailor it as to make it more easily usable by the target audience. Similarly, while remarkable progress had been made in

- digitalising services, these were not very focused on the users, but rather replicated the offline experience.
- Monitoring and evaluation: E-government projects were inconsistently assessed and, when evaluations did take place, they were carried out by comparing outcomes to predetermined targets, without sufficient consideration of broader service performance or unexpected outcomes. In addition, these assessments and the occasional cost-benefit analysis only looked at financial benefits, without sufficient consideration of other social benefits, which can be difficult to measure.

Based on these findings, the OECD Secretariat formulated tailored policy recommendations, with the input of OECD peers, to help Mexico make progress in the implementation of its e-government efforts (Box 2.1).

A little over five years later, the Mexican Ministry of Public Administration partnered again with the OECD to perform a Public Governance Review (OECD, 2011), which included an assessment of the evolution of e-government policies and their state of affairs at the time and advanced recommendations to push the e-government agenda forward in the context of an international financial crisis.

The 2011 Public Governance Review of Mexico highlighted the Mexican government's achievements in advancing the e-government agenda, and in particular its efforts to support greater integration (i.e. Federal Inventory System, International Trade Single Window, integration of RUPA in the Citizens' Portal) and interoperability (i.e. Interoperability Scheme, RUPA, RUV) and improve co-ordination and the institutional set up (adjustments made at the level of the Commission for the Development of e-Government [CIDGE]), advances in the existing legal and regulatory framework of e-government, and in efforts for measuring e-government performance.

However, the Public Governance Review of Mexico also found outstanding challenges that echoed those identified in the 2005 e-Government Study. Indeed, these included:

- A gap in the alignment and articulation of the e-government strategy and other relevant ICT strategies
- despite progress, the co-ordination function of the CIGDE remained relatively weak, which undermined the impact of e-government initiatives, particularly where horizontality and collaboration between stakeholders was required
- uneven technological maturity of public organisations within and across levels of government
- frameworks for ICT project justification and budgeting showed weaknesses and rigidities that could lead to project failures
- the need for upskilling and ensuring desirable talent in key positions and functions for e-government implementation and development
- the need to better share resources and reuse or scale-up existing solutions as appropriate
- insufficient use and analysis of the wealth of data collected in the implementation of ICT projects.

> **Box 2.1. 2005 e-Government Study of Mexico: Key policy recommendations**
>
> 1. Governance and co-ordination:
>   - Strengthen leadership and enhance communication. Put in place an appropriate institutional set-up that reinforces core organisations' capacities in key areas to permit e-government leaders to enable new ways of working; provide e-government leads with direct access to the heads of their respective organisations; develop a communications strategy focused on the reuse of solutions and spread of good practices.
>   - Better integrate the horizontal components of e-government across the Good Government Agenda, identify areas of co-operation and commit to shared responsibility for achieving outcomes.
>   - Promote efficient and effective collaboration, including a fundamental framework for collaboration, practical support and assistance to agencies, use of incentives and sanctions to foster collaboration, and re-examine how budget structures and processes can better enable collaboration.
> 2. Public service delivery and user focus:
>   - Improve service quality regardless of its delivery channel, develop a multi-channel service delivery strategy. Promote seamless service delivery by encouraging institutions to work together to better develop integrated solutions. Promote the development of e government at the local level.
>   - More actively engage citizens on line for policy making and let users know how the results from their involvement affects policy making.
>   - Take steps to establish a single citizen registry to enhance the development of front and back office electronic services.
> 3. Frameworks and capabilities for delivery:
>   - Promote transparent, efficient and flexible IT investments by developing strong business cases and increasing the flexibility of funding arrangements. Simplify and reduce regulatory barriers inside government.
>   - Ensure the skills needed to work in an IT-enabled administration by extending IT training for all public servants and providing updated business skills for managers.
>   - Ensure monitoring systems focus on value for government and users, beyond the achievement of predetermined goals, including the value of collaborative initiatives by developing government-wide outcome measures that can be embedded into individual agencies' plans.
>
> Source: OECD (2005), OECD E-Government Studies: Mexico, https://doi.org/10.1787/9789264010727-en.

Based on this assessment, the OECD Public Governance Review of Mexico advanced a number of policy recommendations for consideration by the Mexican government as a means of making progress in the implementation of e-government (Box 2.2). These recommendations were broadly taken on board despite the changing administration in 2012.

In 2012, the then incoming administration added to Mexico's efforts in the first decade of the 21st century, resulting in a commendable effort in the use of technology "to achieve better government" (OECD, 2014). The commitment to continuous improvement using the world's most digitally advanced countries as a benchmark helped lay the foundations for the government of Mexico to leapfrog its way forward to become a regional and global leader in digital government and open government data (see Chapter 1).

> **Box 2.2. Public Governance Review of Mexico of 2011:**
>
> 1. Governance and co-ordination:
>   - Improve alignment and articulation of the digital government strategy with other relevant ICT strategies.
>   - Consider reinforcing the role of the Commission for the Development of e-Government as the body responsible for ensuring co-ordination in the use of ICT within the federal public administration and across levels of government.
>   - Review funding arrangements and mechanisms for ICT and e government projects to improve the budgetary framework and remove existing barriers.
>   - Create frameworks that foster the adoption, reuse and scale up of existing applications and solutions.
> 2. Enhancing state capability to support e-government implementation:
>   - Make efforts to help public entities achieve a greater level of digital maturity, enabling them to perform in a more advanced digital and integrated environment. Consider extending the Evaluation Model for Digital Government across policy areas and levels of government to map the level of maturity across the whole public administration.
>   - Complement the ICT strategic plans with robust business case models.
>   - Ensure adequate levels of digital skills, knowledge and capacity, in particular in the body responsible for approving e-government projects.
>   - Monitor closely, and optimising the use of, the wealth of results, information and evidence acquired through current projects.
>   - Increase the number of services where the advanced digital signature can be used.

References

OECD (2014), "Recommendation of the Council on Digital Government Strategies", OECD, Paris, https://www.oecd.org/gov/digital-government/Recommendation-digital-government-strategies.pdf.

OECD (2011), Towards More Effective and Dynamic Public Management in Mexico, OECD Public Governance Reviews, OECD Publishing, Paris, https://doi.org/10.1787/9789264116238-en.

OECD (2005), OECD e-Government Studies: Mexico 2005, OECD e-Government Studies, OECD Publishing, Paris, https://doi.org/10.1787/9789264010727-en.

World Bank (2018), World Development Indicators (database), World Bank, Washington, DC, https://datacatalog.worldbank.org/dataset/world-development-indicators.

3 Governance for sustainable and inclusive digital government

Chapter 3 provides an assessment of the governance of digital government in Mexico. It describes and appraises the National Digital Strategy and its structures. Furthermore, this chapter considers the progress made in setting up the enablers of the digital transformation. In addition, this chapter takes in what the digital transformation entails for the political leadership, and how senior leadership in the public sector enable digital government implementation and innovation. The chapter closes with an analysis of the organisational structure and architecture that underpins digital government policy in Mexico.

The statistical data for Israel are supplied by and under the responsibility of the relevant Israeli authorities. The use of such data by the OECD is without prejudice to the status of the Golan Heights, East Jerusalem and Israeli settlements in the West Bank under the terms of international law.

The National Digital Strategy (2013-18)

Since the launch of the OECD Public Governance Review in 2011, the government of Mexico took decisive steps to continue to push forward the digital agenda as a means to achieve better government, economic growth, and social and digital inclusion. Under the 2012-18 federal administration, a new National Digital Strategy (Estrategia Digital Nacional, EDN) was launched, with a clear articulation with the public sector reform programme and the National Development Plan, thus recognising the strategic value of digitalisation for the public sector and society more broadly. The Coordination of the National Digital Strategy office was created under the Office of the President to oversee and co-ordinate the implementation of the EDN.

The Mexican National Development Plan for the 2013-18 period included three cross cutting strategies: 1) democratising productivity; 2) closer and modern government; and 3) gender perspective (Government of Mexico, 2013b). The Closer and Modern Government Programme is structured around 5 objectives which are themselves broken down into 209 lines of action (Government of Mexico, 2013c). The five objectives are to:

1. promote an open government that fosters accountability in the federal public administration (Administración Pública Federal, APF)
2. strengthen results-based budgeting of the APF, including federalised spending
3. optimise the use of the APF's resources
4. improve public management in the APF
5. establish a National Digital Strategy that accelerates Mexico into the information and knowledge society.

By putting digital and data at the centre of its public sector reform efforts, Mexico took consequential steps to embed a new culture in its civil service and prepare the country to better respond to an age of technological disruption.

The EDN, its structure and objectives have a significant focus on improving public sector performance (Government of Mexico, 2013a). It identified five strategic objectives that would drive the digital transformation of government, education, health, the economy and government-citizen relations (Figure 3.1).

As highlighted in the previous chapter, Mexico identified early on the power of digital and has been consistently making efforts to achieve excellence and innovate its public management and service delivery. These efforts have paid off. The country has firmly established itself as a leader in Latin America and the Caribbean and, progressively, the world, as its performance in international metrics show (Figure 3.2).

However, while this success should be seen as a recognition for the work done, it should not lead to complacency. Despite the critical importance of digital disruption, digital strategies often fail (Bughin et al., 2018). The digital transformation implies both innovation in service delivery models and operations driven by a thorough understanding of digital economics, including scale, network effects, near-zero marginal costs, ecosystem approaches and the value delivered to the user.

Governments often operate in political environments of competing interests and changing policy priorities, but the digital transformation of government demands sustained effort. Effective governance in the 21st century will require governments to embed advancements in analytics into public sector operations, at all levels and sectors, to draw new insights, enable smart automation where valuable, develop new business models and make public policy more effective. The digital disruption has barely started, and it is likely to accelerate. Deprioritising the digital transformation of the public sector or overseeing the current and upcoming challenges could result in significant failures in the Mexican public sector. This study seeks to flag these potential pitfalls for the Mexican government and encourage constructive and informed action going forward.

Figure 3.1. Structure of the Mexican National Digital Strategy: Objectives and enablers

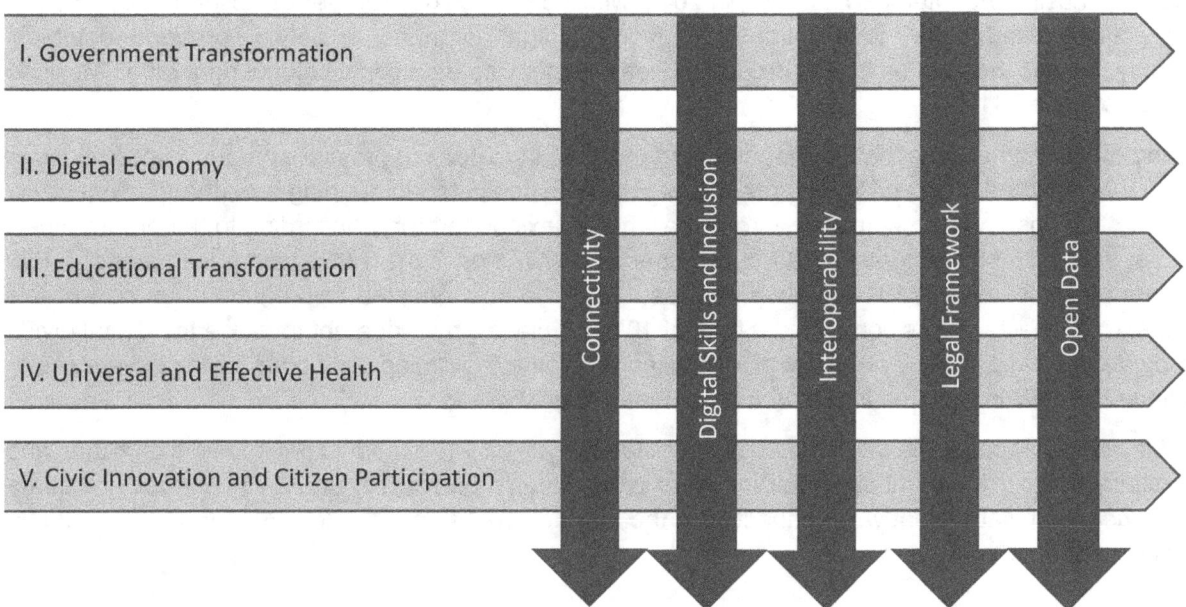

Source: Government of Mexico (2013a), Estrategia Nacional Digital, https://www.gob.mx/mexicodigital.

Figure 3.2. Mexico's performance in international indices on digital government

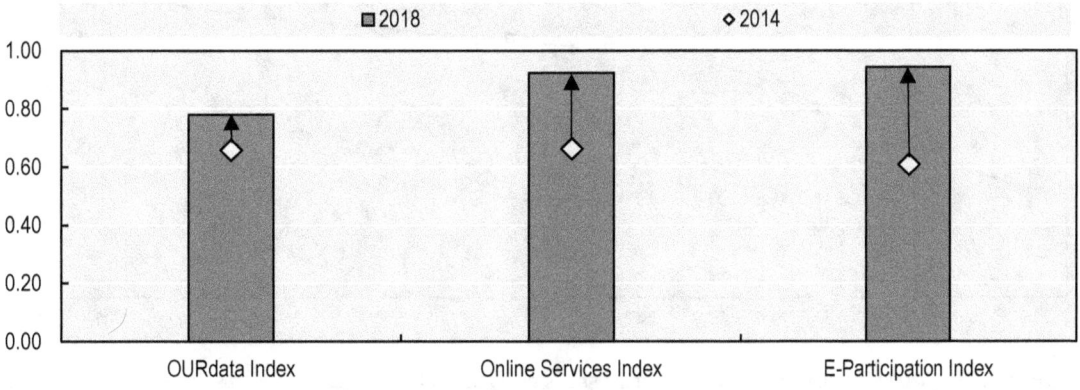

Source: OECD (2018a), Open Government Data Report: Enhancing Policy Maturity for Sustainable Impact, https://doi.org/10.1787/9789264305847-en; UNDESA (2018), "E-Government Survey".

The enablers of the digital transformation

Mexico's National Digital Strategy relies on five enablers that will make the transformation possible. This section will provide a brief overview of the efforts made and the areas of opportunity for Mexico going forward.

Connectivity

Access to basic ICT infrastructure, and notably the Internet, is the enabler and backbone of the digital revolution. By this metric, Mexico has performed below the OECD average, with a relatively low share of the population using the Internet. However, in 2013, Mexico took bold, courageous action to address this challenge and accelerate the country's transition towards a digital economy, society and government. Most remarkably, access to the Internet and broadband was recognised as a constitutional right for all Mexican citizens as of June 2013[1].

By setting the right to access the Internet, the government of Mexico put pressure on public institutions to live up to this standard. Mexico Conectado[2] is a programme dedicated to bringing broadband connectivity to public institutions and public spaces across the whole Mexican territory. According to the programme's indicators, so far 68 806 schools, 9 935 public spaces, 9 757 hospitals, 6 033 community areas, 6 690 government institutions and 101 research centres[3] have been connected to broadband as part of this effort. Mexico Conectado has connected a total of 101 322 places in an attempt to tackle the digital divide and improve coverage. The government also focused on creating enabling conditions for the private sector to continue to invest in required infrastructure to enable digitalisation.

While Mexico still scores below the OECD average (Figure 3.3), it has experienced significant and accelerating growth in the number of Internet users in the country, particularly after 2014. Indeed, the share of the Mexican population that was connected to the Internet went from 44.4% in 2014 to 57.4% in 2015, and has continued to grow since.

Figure 3.3. Internet users as share of the total population

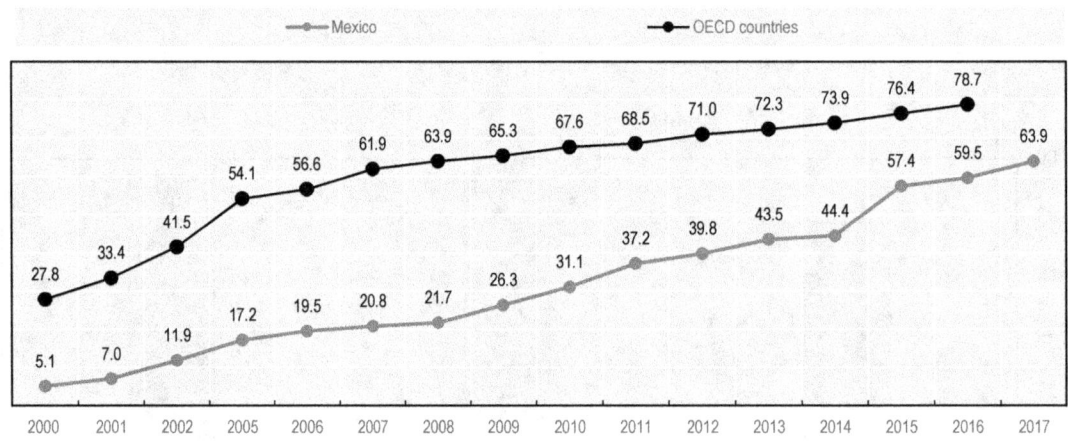

Source: World Bank (2018), World Development Indicators (database), https://datacatalog.worldbank.org/dataset/world-development-indicators.

Mobile subscriptions per 100 inhabitants has experienced even faster growth than the number of Internet users (Figure 3.4). However, its growth rate has stalled comparatively in recent years, falling substantively behind OECD peers and countries from Latin America and the Caribbean (Figure 3.4).

Figure 3.4. Mobile subscriptions per 100 inhabitants

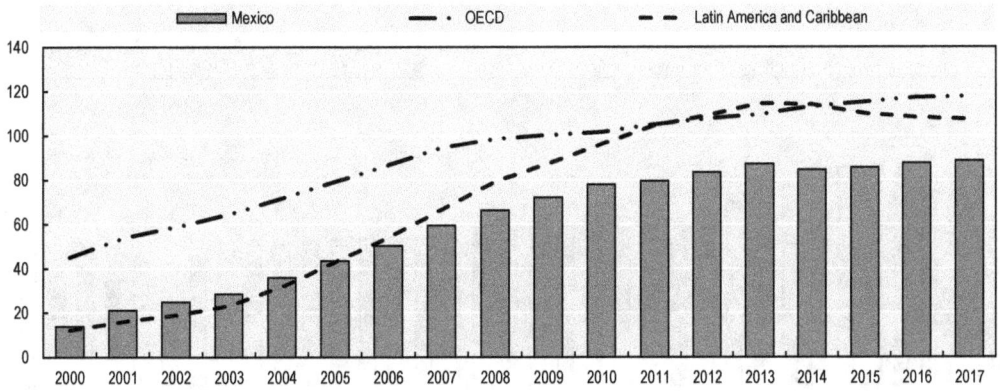

Source: World Bank (2018), World Development Indicators (database), https://datacatalog.worldbank.org/dataset/world-development-indicators.

While Mexico has made substantial progress, the development and adoption of key strategic infrastructure to support the new digital revolution is an area of opportunity requiring special attention. This is particularly true for the case of broadband. Indeed, Mexico comes next to last in terms of fixed broadband subscriptions among OECD countries (Figure 3.5). It also performs poorly in terms of mobile broadband subscriptions, topping only Greece, Hungary and Colombia among its peers (Figure 3.6). From a digital government perspective, Mexico would do well to double down on its efforts to expand connectivity and inclusion, as it would allow the country to reap the full benefits from public sector transformation and the digitalisation of the economy and society.

Figure 3.5. OECD fixed broadband subscriptions per 100 inhabitants, by technology, December 2017

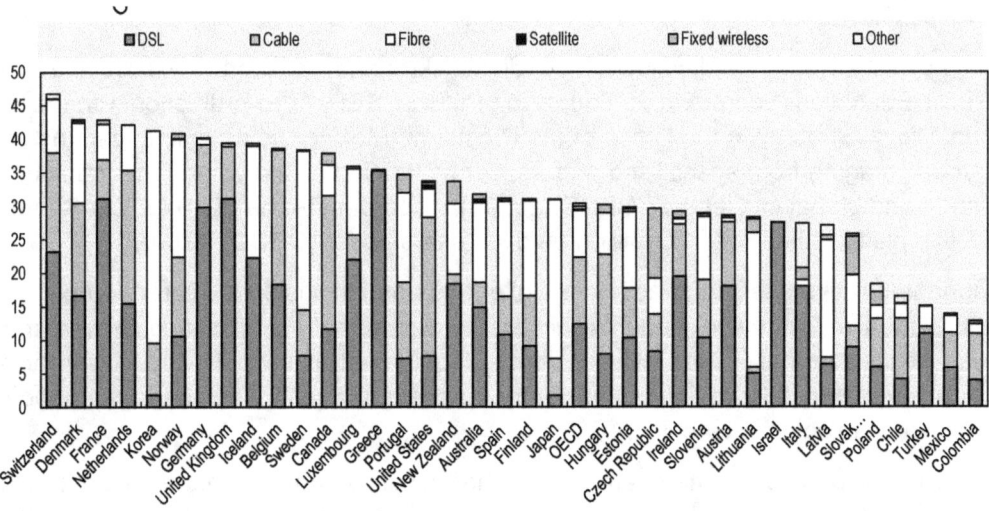

Notes: Canada: fixed wireless includes satellite. France: cable includes VDSL2 THD. Germany: cable includes HFC lines; fibre includes fibre lines provided by cable operators; fixed wireless includes BWA subscribers; other includes leased lines. Israel: temporary OECD estimates. Italy: terrestrial fixed wireless data include WiMax lines; other includes vDSL services. Switzerland and United States: data for December 2017 are estimates. Information on data for Israel: http://oe.cd/israel-disclaimer.
Source: OECD Broadband Portal, www.oecd.org/sti/broadband/oecdbroadbandportal.htm.

Figure 3.6. OECD mobile broadband subscriptions per 100 inhabitants, by technology, December 2017

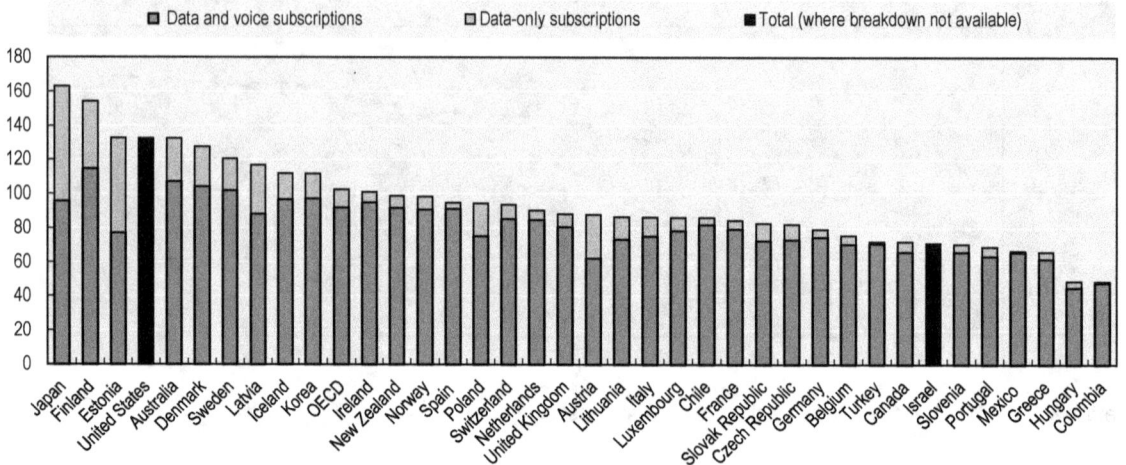

Notes: Israel: temporary OECD estimates. Switzerland: data for December 2017 are estimates. United States: data from Ovum. Information on data for Israel: http://oe.cd/israel-disclaimer.
Source: OECD Broadband Portal, www.oecd.org/sti/broadband/oecdbroadbandportal.htm.

Digital skills and inclusion

Building the digital skills of society can help drive innovation in the production of goods and services as well as their adoption, use and consumption by members of society, thus enabling new business models. The National Digital Strategy (EDN) points to social inclusion and the development of digital skills as critical factors making digital success possible in the country. Flagship initiatives like Prospera Digital (Box 3.1) are proof of these efforts.

MéxicoX[4] is a key initiative on the development of digital skills and inclusion in Mexico. Developed by the Ministry of Public Education (Secretaría de Educación Pública, SEP) in co-ordination with the Coordination of the National Digital Strategy in the Office of the President, MéxicoX is an online learning platform with over 230 courses, ranging from specialised and academic training all the way to the training of teachers, national, cultural and global challenges (OECD, 2018b). According to the 2018 OECD Survey on Digital Government, this platform has over 1.5 million enrolled users so far (OECD, 2018b).

Another important initiative seeking to advance digital skills and inclusion is @prende.mx.[5] This initiative has run pilots aimed at improving students' access to digital technologies and their responsible and conscious use of the Internet. It has also enhanced equipment in schools and classrooms with new technologies while creating a learning community for teachers facilitating the sharing of good practices in the use of digital technologies in teaching.

While the initiative is promising, there are many shortcomings that still need to be addressed. The programme has yet to develop indicators of success to understand its impact on broader education outcomes or skills development. Moreover, it is unclear whether the measures aimed at fostering the use of digital technologies in the education process are robust enough to instil a digital and innovation culture among teachers.

> **Box 3.1. Leveraging new technologies to foster inclusion with Prospera Digital**
>
> Prospera Digital is one of the flagship initiatives of the Mexican government using new technologies to help advance social inclusion. The initiative has sought to transform the largest social programme in Mexico and the second largest conditioned cash transfer in the world using user-centred design, digital delivery systems and data-driven strategies.
>
> The initiative, led by Prospera and the National Bank of Savings and Financial Services with the support of the Coordination of the National Digital Strategy and other relevant stakeholders, consisted in the following:
>
> - User research: interviews, surveys and field research to identify the need for tailored digital financial products and education to help advance financial inclusion.
> - Intervention design: including delivery systems and financial education modules and materials.
> - Experimentation: A series of pilots are being run using randomised controlled trials to test different digital systems (mobile applications and debit cards) to deliver benefits, complemented with a financial education programme and application, providing relevant information to support households' financial decisions. Mobile solutions also provide mothers with critical maternal health advice.
> - Scale up: Based on the results of these pilots, tailored solutions and digital delivery systems and interfaces will be scaled up, potentially reaching 7 million households, or roughly 30 million Mexicans.
>
> Sources: OECD (2015), "Digital government toolkit: Good practices – Prospera Digital", www.oecd.org/gov/mexico-prospera-digital.pdf(accessed on 26 October 2018); https://www.gob.mx/mexicodigital/articulos/prospera-digital-inclusion-financiera; UNICEF (2015), "The case of Prospera Digital", http://unicefstories.org/2015/11/18/the-case-of-prospera-digital-digital-tools-and-data-driven-strategies-to-transform-the-largest-social-program-in-mexico-part-2 (accessed on 26 October 2018); Coordination of the National Digital Strategy (2018), "National Digital Strategy – Project files", unpublished.

It is, however, a sign of hope that Mexico recognises these shortcomings and is taking steps to address these issues and make educational transformation viable and sustainable. It is working with other countries from Latin America and the Caribbean to strengthen the use of ICTs in the education sector, overall digital skills and computational thinking in their respective countries

An additional critique that could be raised against this programme is that insufficient attention is paid to low-skilled workers that will increasingly face pressures to reskill and upskill to acquire at the very least basic digital skills. The rise of automation makes this all the more relevant and urgent. The digital strategy should push relevant stakeholders in government to focus on identifying particularly vulnerable groups and take action early. The transition towards broad automation may after all take place more rapidly than we expect.

Interoperability

The focus on enhancing interoperability as a driver of government business process and service delivery transformation is one of the key bets of the Mexican government and rightly so. The Mexican single portal, Gob.mx, with the support of a new normative framework for digital government, has been driving interoperability between sectors and government departments. In addition, the initiative InteroperaMX[6] a platform facilitating the sharing of reliable data, has been an outstanding achievement in fostering data sharing and interoperability within the public sector.

InteroperaMX, inspired by the Estonian X-Road, is a platform that allows public institutions to share reliable and trustworthy data, with clear identification of the source and certification of the information. The driver for this effort is the vision for a public administration where the user only has to provide information once to the public sector (once only principle).

The birth certificate is the use case chosen by the government to illustrate the power of InteroperaMX and thus of interoperability in the public sector. A birth certificate is required as proof of identity for 2 210 or 46% of all public procedures and services at the federal level. To grasp the high impact of this use case it is important to keep in mind that 45% of completed government transactions in Mexico concern proofs of identity and civil registration (IDB, 2018). In its analogue format, the birth certificate has a considerable financial impact in terms of explicit and implicit costs for the citizen (money and time investments), in particular for those with the lowest income. The government of Mexico estimates that Mexican citizens invested MXN 2.2 billion in 2016 (approximately USD 115.5 million), with the poorest 10% spending roughly 1.5% of their real annual income. These estimates do not include costs related to transportation, bribery or time spent to complete the procedure.[7]

So far, 2.75 million birth certificates have been downloaded.[8] Thanks to InteroperaMX, Mexico now benefits from 8 certified trusted sources, 65 services use the Single Identity Number for the Population Registry (Clave Única del Registro de Población, CURP)[9], 150 services that are interoperable with the birth certificate and ID, and 450 services that are interoperable with the Mexican digital signature (e.firma).[10]

Interoperability and digital identity are considered key enablers of the digital transformation as these components facilitate the secure sharing of data to help the public sector to reliably determine the identity, duties and entitlements of service users. These initiatives have enormous potential to drive transformation both within the public sector and outside of it by enabling digital delivery models. However, they so far lack scale or sufficient transparency around the use and sharing of personal data by public institutions. This final point is one that could and should be considered for future iterations (Box 3.2).

Box 3.2. Carpeta Ciudadana (citizen file): Enhancing data management and service delivery in Spain

The Spanish administration has implemented the "Carpeta Ciudadana", or citizen file. Carpeta Ciudadana provides citizens with a simple and agile single point of access to gain information on their open files and procedures with the Spanish public administration. Citizens can also directly contact the public institutions responsible for following up on such files to obtain more information.

Carpeta Ciudadana also provides citizens with information on their personal data currently held by the public administration and what institutions currently have the citizens' consent to use specific data. The platform allows the citizen to trace the sharing of data that concerns him/her between public institutions. As of June 2017, Carpeta Ciudadana included the participation of a limited number of services and public institutions, but ongoing efforts exist to significantly increase the number of services included in this platform.

The current version of the citizen file is being reviewed in view of revamping the platform to include new functionalities. In particular, a future version would allow the users to know exactly what their data have been used for.

Source: Government of Spain (n.d.), "Carpeta Ciudadana", webpage (in Spanish), https://administracionelectronica.gob.es/ctt/ccd#.WT6NkG995hE (accessed on 9 February 2018); and internal documents from the 2017 E-Leaders' Thematic Group on Personal Data Ownership and Transparency

Legal framework

The legal and regulatory framework for digital government and ICTs is an inevitable component of adjusting governance to the digital age. In this domain, Mexico has also taken significant steps in this direction. Following the above-mentioned constitutional reform, Article 6, in its third paragraph, of the Mexican Constitution now reads:

> *The state will guarantee the right to free access to information and communications technologies, as well as broadcasting and telecommunication services, including broadband and the Internet. For these purposes, the state will establish conditions for effective competition in the provision of those services.*

Indeed, the 2012-18 Peña Nieto administration has focused important energies on fostering competition in the telecommunications sector. It has also pushed for a modernisation of the regulatory and normative framework governing digital government.

The current legal and regulatory framework of digital government in Mexico provides a framework for the progressive digital integration of the federal public administration (APF). Indeed, the APF has progressively established procedures that facilitate the sharing of digital documents and data to avoid duplications across public services for business[11] and individual users[12] (OECD, 2018b). The APF Agreement on Interoperability and Open Data[13] sets the framework for data, semantic, organisational and technical interoperability, further specified in the technical guidelines and standards.[14]

Furthermore, the modernisation of the legal and regulatory framework has also sought to ensure better standards for procuring technology in the public sector, including the use of cloud computing, open source software, as well as structuring ICT projects and ensuring cybersecurity of government systems (OECD, 2018b). The General Law on Personal Data Protection[15] has brought greater clarity to the existing legal and regulatory framework on privacy protection in Mexico. [16]

Substantial efforts have also been made to establish a clear regulatory framework[17] for open government data along with supporting implementation guides[18] (OECD, 2018c), and to provide the necessary legal conditions for the adoption of the advanced electronic signature[19] and digital identification mechanisms.[20] In addition, new rules and regulations exist for the management of digital documents[21] and a National Cybersecurity Strategy has been established.[22]

These changes should be welcome and encouraged. They provide a framework that enables more joined-up and data-driven approaches in the implementation of digital government. However, more is needed for these approaches to be streamlined and ingrained in the fabric of government as default ways of working. More importantly, the digital disruption will continue to raise new issues, challenge conventional thinking and approaches, which will push existing frameworks to the edge and require regulators and policy makers alike to rethink the rules governing the system. As the government of Mexico seeks to enhance service delivery through digital approaches, it seems of critical importance that frameworks such as those dedicated to ICT commissioning are revised to support digital technologies and methodologies (see Chapter 3).

Open government data

Data, including open government data (OGD), is a strategic enabler of the digital transformation that allows government to work as a platform for the co-creation of public value (OECD, 2018a). OGD is driven by digital era values and principles of openness and transparency. Open-by-default standards give governments the opportunity to leverage outside talent and capabilities not only to help advance government accountability, but also public sector performance and social and economic innovations that deliver convenient new services.

In 2016 the government of Mexico, through the Coordination of the National Digital Strategy, the General Direction of Open Data and the Ministry of Public Administration partnered with the OECD to perform an

OECD Open Government Data Review of Mexico (OECD, 2016b). The review provided an assessment of open government data policies in Mexico in the light of the OECD analytical framework for open government data (Ubaldi, 2013) and international best practices. The review highlighted opportunities for Mexico to reap the full benefits of OGD and continue to advance towards a strategic use of data to support the digital transformation of government, society and the economy.

Most notably, the OECD review advanced the following recommendations:

Governance: Building a pro-open data public sector
1. Sustain the co-ordination of the OGD policy implementation between the Office of the President and other relevant institutions (e.g. the SFP).
2. Ensure availability and continuity of federal funding for open data policy.
3. Develop a structured National Open Data Strategy driven by the needs of the Mexican ecosystem.
4. Support the definition and publication of a single legal instrument covering all regulations and guidelines covering personal data protection.
5. Ensure the continuity of technical support bodies providing guidance to public institutions in line with OGD policy.
6. Highlight the relevance of chief data officers within public institutions.
7. Foster government-to-government collaboration between public institutions.

Towards a demand- and value-driven data disclosure
1. Run regular consultation exercises with different user groups.
2. Update the central OGD portal into a data request and data co-creation platform.
3. Support line ministries to connect with users of their data.

Building skills of user communities
1. Provide capacity building for broader society and specific user groups.
2. Use Retos Públicos as a two-way data exchange platform.
3. Leverage Retos Públicos to build the capacities of public institutions to engage with user communities.

Open data and data-driven economy
1. Perform exercises to identify business-oriented data demand.
2. Leverage the networks of the Ministry of Economy to develop a data-driven economy.
3. Develop partnerships with academia to stimulate data-driven entrepreneurship.

Towards a data-driven public sector
1. Utilise open data reuse and its potential for organisational efficiency by improving G2G data-sharing.
2. Involve public officials in the design and implementation of OGD policies.
3. Use Open Data Squads to build institutional capacities and co-ordination on data analytics' efforts.

Open data at the local level
1. Expand the areas of work of the Open Mexico Network to increase its relevance for local communities.
2. Sustain multi-level collaboration through the Open Mexico Network.
3. Leverage the Open Mexico Network to (1) strengthen horizontal collaboration between local governments and (2) further connect local governments with the international open data ecosystem.
4. Co-ordinate with local governments to further reach stakeholders at the local level for greater value co-creation.

The 2016 Open Government Data Review of Mexico benefited from a follow-up project in 2018 to assess the progress made since the publication of the review in terms of implementation. The study provided a general overview of the state of implementation of the recommendations advanced in the 2016 review (Figure 3.7).

Figure 3.7. Results of the 2018 OECD Open Government Data Review of Mexico: General summary

	Fully achieved	Ongoing actions	Discussions underway on course of action	Pending discussions
Governance: Building a pro-open-data public sector				
Recommendation 1		●		
Recommendation 2		●		
Recommendation 3			●	
Recommendation 4		●		
Recommendation 5		●		
Recommendation 6				●
Recommendation 7	●			
Towards a demand -and value-driven data disclosure				
Recommendation 1	●			
Recommendation 2	●			
Recommendation 3		●		
Building skills across external social user communities and engaging the ecosystem				
Recommendation 1	●			
Recommendation 2	●			
Recommendation 3	●			
Open data and the data-driven economy				
Recommendation 1	●			
Recommendation 2	●			
Recommendation 3				●
Towards a data-driven public sector				
Recommendation 1		●		
Recommendation 2	●			
Recommendation 3	●			
Recommendation 4		●		
Open data at the local level				
Recommendation 1	●			
Recommendation 2	●			
Recommendation 3	●			
Recommendation 4	●			
Total	14	7	1	2

In addition, the 2018 report assessed the present environment to make forward-looking recommendations that would help the government of Mexico make strategic choices today so that the national OGD ecosystem continues to grow in maturity and robustness (OECD, 2018c). The study focused on assessing the overarching frameworks that would support a sustained effort in setting up open data as an enabler or infrastructure for the digital transformation of the Mexican society. It particular, it encouraged the Mexican government to:

- formalise the positions of chief data officer and chief digital transformation officer and consider the establishment of a digitalisation agency responsible for co ordinating the country's digital agenda
- ensure the regular flow of funds to implement open data policy and initiatives

- strengthen the national legal framework for open government data to support policy continuity and set clear regulations and improve capacities within public sector institutions to make data available and accessible
- develop a dedicated national open data roadmap, in line with the overall national digital agenda, the National Digital Strategy
- further connect open data initiatives with other sectoral policies and sustain the current efforts to use open data for anti-corruption, public procurement of major infrastructure projects, natural risk management and social inclusion
- support the appointment of institutional chief data officers in line ministries and ensure inter-institutional collaboration through horizontal co-ordination bodies
- develop open data understanding, skills and capacities across the public sector
- develop data architecture and data governance models for the public sector, and connect these efforts to the overall open data policy
- continue efforts to strengthen the value of the MX Open Data Infrastructure (IDMX) for all actors and for policy sustainability
- improve the usefulness and user-friendliness of the central open data portal; build capacities among key partners such as journalists and civil society organisations
- enable collective efforts to map the open data ecosystem
- involve major private sector players in order to make the business case for open data in Mexico and explore the implementation of government-led seed funding.

This recent assessment by the OECD remains valid today and relevant as Mexico seeks to push forward and mature the open government data in the country.

Political leadership: Creating an enabling environment for change

To drive the transformation, the government of Mexico must take bold action and make the digital government efforts sustainable in the long term. Securing the right level of political support and leadership is fundamental in this respect.

Successful digital strategies in the public sector need political sponsors that are willing to challenge organisations' status quo bias (Bracken and Greenway, 2018). Leadership is a key component in all reform and change management strategies, but digital disruption is putting additional pressure on political leaders and senior managers to be and remain engaged.

At a fundamental level, political leaders create the authorising environment that allows digital leaders in the public sector to take action and drive change within and across institutions. It is the political support that empowers the public administration to act against legacy systems and settled interest groups (i.e. traditional public sector IT providers unwilling to adjust). Political leadership also helps convene relevant stakeholders to work together towards a common goal (Andrews, Pritchett and Woolcock, 2017).

In addition, political leaders and senior managers are responsible for setting the public sector's or their organisation's strategic direction. Successful digital transformation of the public sector must: leverage digital strategies and technologies to support public policy objectives; and transform the public sector processes, operating models and service delivery arrangements.

Setting organisational strategies in the digital age has become increasingly challenging for political leaders and chief executives. To appropriately understand the strategic choices at hand, public sector leadership has little choice but to become familiar with the notions around emerging technologies to grasp their strategic implications (Díaz, Rowshankish and Saleh, 2018).

Senior executives must understand how new tools, like artificial intelligence, machine learning algorithms, the Internet of Things (IoT) or blockchain could impact their sectors and organisations. Only this will set them up for success, allowing them to take sound decisions as they set out to develop, endorse and push a shared vision for their organisation(s) going forward. Yet, digital is also increasingly likely to raise sensitive political and ethical questions. Digital success in the public sector will thus need growing involvement of high-level political leadership, which is both inevitable and desirable.

International experiences highlight that successful digital government strategies need political sponsorship that is able to drive change across government institutions and functions (Bracken and Greenway, 2018; Bracken et al., 2018). Transforming government requires the mobilisation of a myriad of actors, networks, structures and systems, which demands substantial political capability. Because of these requirements in terms of political leverage, digital government authorities are very often located at a central department or ministry, close or within the centre of government, with a transversal mandate such as a cabinet office, Ministry of Finance or the Ministry of Public Administration. It is no coincidence that 30 out of 37 OECD countries and 18 out of the top 20 governments in the UN eGovernment Index have located their digital government authority in cross-cutting or transversal ministries. This is also consistent with previous OECD work on the comparative governance and leadership of digital government (OECD, 2016a).

Mexico has successfully adopted a model where the political push comes from the centre, the Coordination of the National Digital Strategy located at the Office of the President, and the implementing drive and support comes from the Ministry of Public Administration. In the past six years, this couple, led by the Coordination of the National Digital Strategy, has been able to support digital government reform, most notably by:

- securing the political capital and support for implementation
- helping bring clarity and definition to the shared vision embodied in the National Digital Strategy
- convening, connecting and engaging critical stakeholders throughout the policy cycle, helping align interests and efforts in favour of successful implementation
- strategic staffing and building capabilities to support the strategic objectives and delivery
- motivating and inspiring stakeholders responsible for delivery
- nurturing a culture of digital innovation in government.

Measured by the rate of digitalisation of public services, this model has delivered. As highlighted in Chapters 1 and 2, Mexico has consolidated itself as a regional leader when it comes to the level of digitalisation of government transactions (IDB, 2018; OECD, 2018b). However, this model is not without its shortcomings.

One key weakness of the current Mexican model is that a disproportionate level of the political drive – and thus the ability to exert influence across sectors – depends on individual executives within the President's Office, who might often struggle to find the time required to effectively drive the digitalisation agenda (Bracken and Greenway, 2018). Experience shows that while digital agendas operated from the office of the head of government or head of state can be extremely effective, they also risk becoming too closely associated with a specific executive or political leader. This means that the digital agenda risks losing relevance every time the individual in question moves on to a new role or the administration changes. The current Mexican model provides no certain answer for the need to ensure sustained efforts in digital government implementation.

There is thus a paradox that appears to need solving: namely, the tension between the need for a political push from the centre and the risk of insufficient attention due to competing priorities within the Office of the President.

Several of the most digitally advanced OECD countries have attempted to solve this tension by creating a dedicated agency for digitalisation with a dedicated senior executive reporting directly to an institution with the necessary political clout to drive government-wide change, such as President's Office or a Ministry of

Finance (OECD, 2016a). This type of arrangement has provided digitalisation agencies with the necessary political support to achieve transversal reform, establish agile and collaborative approaches across the administration, and create incentives that support cultural change. The mandate to focus on digitalisation has often ensured adequate levels of accountability, specialisation and a reasonable scope for organisational performance assessment. Just as importantly, these digitalisation agencies have had the budget, convening and enforcement power required to accelerate the development of a robust and dynamic digital ecosystem, thus providing for sustained and effective efforts in government transformation.

Organisational frameworks to deliver on digital ambitions

The challenge of enabling and sustaining the digital transformation of the public sector is more than technical, that is to say, mostly cultural, organisational and political. The key question is: how does the public sector get organised to deliver on its digital ambitions? The answer to this question, as in all governance and political questions, is largely contextual. It depends on the specific characteristics of the problem; the written and unwritten rules of the operating environment; and the political, economic and social variables underpinning institutional arrangements. However, broad lessons can be drawn from international experiences and success stories (OECD, 2014, 2016a; n.d.).

> **Box 3.3. Digitalisation agencies in Portugal and Denmark**
>
> Given the complexity and the disruptive potential of digitalisation and the redesigning of government functioning and operations, to achieve its goals the unit or function in charge of such a feat must count on strong political support and commitment and the ability to drive cross-sector transformation. Locating the digital government authority in close proximity to powerful government institutions (e.g. centre of government, Ministry of Finance) provides it with significant political clout, while ensuring that its leadership is focused on its role and mandate.
>
> For instance, the Portuguese Administrative Modernisation Agency, an executive agency, is located at the Presidency of the Council of Ministers and has substantive powers in terms of allocation of financial resources and approval of ICT projects. The Administrative Modernisation Agency manages the administrative modernisation financing programme, which is composed of EU structural funds and national resources. This gives the agency important leverage to ensure the implementation as the approval of funding for digital government projects through this programme is conditioned on compliance with existing guidelines and standards. Similarly, every ICT project of EUR 10 000 or more must be approved by the operational e-government network that is chaired by the Administrative Modernisation Agency. This network verifies compliance with guidelines, the non-duplication of efforts, and compares prices and budgets with previous projects in order to ensure the best value for money.
>
> Similarly, the Danish Agency for Digitalisation sits under the Ministry of Finance, which under the annual budget negotiations verifies that the agency's guidelines, standards and strategic directions are being followed before granting budget to any digitalisation initiative or programme. It has also helped drive the digitalisation agenda thanks to its broad political influence and focus on efficiency and productivity gains for the public sector.
>
> Source: OECD (2016a), Digital Government in Chile: Strengthening the Institutional and Governance Framework, http://dx.doi.org/10.1787/9789264258013-en.

Since 2001, Mexico has progressively taken steps to improve the organisational structures supporting its public sector digitalisation and modernisation efforts. The partnership between the now extinct President's Government Innovation Office (and subsequently the Coordination of the National Digital Strategy, operating today at the Office of the President) and the Ministry of Public Administration has allowed the government of Mexico to achieve more robust integration of digital efforts, from connectivity to digital economy and society as well as government transformation. It also secured enough political capital to launch an ambitious, mission-driven initiative to overhaul the government services portal. As a result, Mexico's Gob.mx, a single window for government services and digital public participation, is widely regarded as an international good practice.

As the Mexican government becomes more digitally mature and sophisticated and digitally driven disruption accelerates, the question that should be asked is whether these arrangements will suffice to ensure continued, government-wide digital development in Mexico.

Digital government policy and implementation co-ordination has been pushed forward by the National Digital Strategy and its Coordination office at the Office of the President; an increasingly robust legal and regulatory framework; and a set of standards, guidelines and toolkits that have allowed the public administration to increasingly harmonise processes and procedures in the APF. Furthermore, the Executive Council Inter-ministerial Commission for e-Government Development (Comisión Intersecretarial para el Desarrollo del Gobierno Electrónico, CIDGE) has ensured technical and operational co-ordination of the implementation of the strategy. The sub-commissions and technical teams of the CIDGE have proved to be critical in the operationalisation of key components of the National Digital Strategy, including digital identity and signature, open data, strategic ICT commissioning and interoperability, among others.

However, while these mechanisms have brought Mexico a long way in terms of technical co-ordination, their limitations become evident when it comes to high-level political co ordination and implementation. The highest ranking co-ordination body for digital government implementation, the CIDGE, meets only at the level of heads of ICT units.[23] While this co-ordination structure has been tremendously successful so far, it is unclear whether it will be sufficient going forward.

Given that digital decisions will inevitably become more intertwined with organisation-wide strategic and political decisions (see above), a space or body for high-level inter institutional co-ordination and strategic orientation on digital matters beyond ad hoc deliberation becomes increasingly necessary. In such a context, the political leadership and the heads of digital teams across the public sector would both be empowered by working closer together and more effectively if they are to effectively push the Mexican federal public administration into worldwide digital leadership.

Indeed, digital transformation implies putting digital opportunities at the core of organisational and government strategy. A change of mind-set is needed to cease seeing technology as merely a support function and come to appreciate it as a highly strategic one. Taking that premise to its logical conclusion means bringing digital out of ICT units into high-level policy discussions.

The analysis of technological trends and the current political dynamics in digital government policy seems to have two main implications: 1) set up a high-level collegial body for the strategic inter-institutional co-ordination of digital government across the federal public administration. This latter body would not replace the very much needed implementation co-ordination level that brings together the leaders of ICT units across the federal administration, but would be a new level of governance meeting at a ministerial or head of agency level; 2) Mexico might benefit from establishing more direct relationships between the digital leaders or digital transformation officers and the political leadership of their respective institutions.

References

Andrews, M., L. Pritchett and M. Woolcock (2017), Building State Capability: Evidence, Analysis, Action. Oxford University Press, Oxford.

Bracken, M. and Greenway, A. (2018), How to Achieve and Sustain Government Digital Transformation, Inter-American Development Bank, Washington, DC, http://dx.doi.org/10.18235/0001215.

Bracken, M. et al. (2018), Digital Transformation at Scale: Why the Strategy is Delivery, London Publishing Partnership, London.

Bughin, J. et al. (2018), "Why digital strategies fail", McKinsey Quarterly, January, https://www.mckinsey.com/business-functions/digital-mckinsey/our-insights/why-digital-strategies-fail.

Coordination of the National Digital Strategy (2018), "National Digital Strategy – Project files", unpublished.

Díaz, A., K. Rowshankish and T. Saleh (2018), "Why data culture matters", McKinsey Quarterly, September, https://www.mckinsey.com/business-functions/mckinsey-analytics/our-insights/why-data-culture-matters.

Government of Mexico (2013a), Estrategia Digital Nacional, Presidencia de los Estados Unidos Mexicanos.

Government of Mexico (2013b), Plan Nacional de Desarrollo de México 2013-2018.

Government of Mexico (2013c), Programa para un Gobierno Cercano y Moderno. Presidencia de los Estados Unidos Mexicanos.

Government of Spain (n.d.), "Carpeta Ciudadana", webpage (in Spanish), https://administracionelectronica.gob.es/ctt/ccd#.WT6NkG995hE.

IDB (2018), Wait No More: Citizens, Red Tape and Digital Government, Roseth, B., a. Reyes and C. Santiso (eds.), Inter-American Development Bank, Washington, DC, https://publications.iadb.org/handle/11319/8930.

OECD (2018a), Open Government Data Report: Enhancing Policy Maturity for Sustainable Impact, OECD Digital Government Studies, OECD Publishing, Paris, http://dx.doi.org/10.1787/9789264305847-en.

OECD (2018b), "Digital Government Survey 2018", OECD, Paris.

OECD (2018c), Open Government Data in Mexico: The Way Forward, OECD Publishing, Paris, https://doi.org/10.1787/9789264297944-en.

OECD (2016a), Digital Government in Chile: Strengthening the Institutional and Governance Framework, OECD Publishing, Paris, https://doi.org/10.1787/9789264258013-en.

OECD (2016b), Open Government Data Review of Mexico: Data Reuse for Public Sector Impact and Innovation, OECD Publishing, Paris, https://doi.org/10.1787/9789264259270-en.

OECD (2015), "Digital government toolkit: Good practices – Prospera Digital", OECD, Paris, www.oecd.org/gov/mexico-prospera-digital.pdf (accessed on 26 October 2018).

OECD (2014), "Recommendation of the Council on Digital Government Strategies", OECD, Paris, https://www.oecd.org/gov/digital-government/Recommendation-digital-government-strategies.pdf.

OECD (n.d.), "The digital transformation of the public sector: Helping governments respond to the needs of networked societies", OECD, Paris.

Ubaldi, B. (2013), "Open government data: Towards empirical analysis of open government data initiatives", OECD Working Papers on Public Governance, No. 22, OECD Publishing, Paris, http://dx.doi.org/10.1787/5k46bj4f03s7-en.

UNDESA (2018), "E-Government Survey", United Nations Department of Economic and Social Affairs.

UNICEF (2015), "The case of Prospera Digital", United Nations International Children's Emergency Fund http://unicefstories.org/2015/11/18/the-case-of-prospera-digital-digital-tools-and-data-driven-strategies-to-transform-the-largest-social-program-in-mexico-part-2 (accessed on 26 October 2018).

World Bank (2018) World Development Indicators (database), World Bank, Washington, DC, https://datacatalog.worldbank.org/dataset/world-development-indicators.

Notes

[1] www.ordenjuridico.gob.mx/Constitucion/articulos/6.pdf.

[2] https://www.mexicoconectado.gob.mx.

[3] https://www.mexicoconectado.gob.mx/?page_id=12786.

[4] www.mexicox.gob.mx.

[5] https://www.gob.mx/cms/uploads/attachment/file/171123/PROGRAMA__APRENDE.pdf.

[6] https://www.gob.mx/interoperabilidad.

[7] Government estimates are captured on an internal assessment of the birth certificate project and are based on 2016 data. The data used for the analysis come from the National Population Registry, average costs of birth certificates as provided by the 32 Mexican states as issued by Ministries of Finance or equivalent institutions, and annual revenue of the first income decile.

[8] According to Google Analytics as of 7 September 2018.

[9] https://www.gob.mx/curp.

[10] https://www.gob.mx/efirma.

[11] www.diputados.gob.mx/LeyesBiblio/pdf/112_180518.pdf.

[12] www.dof.gob.mx/nota_detalle.php?codigo=5380863&fecha=03/02/2015.

[13] http://dof.gob.mx/nota_detalle.php?codigo=5208001&fecha=06/09/2011.

[14] https://www.gob.mx/interoperabilidad/es/articulos/guias-tecnicas-de-interoperabilidad?idiom=es.

[15] www.diputados.gob.mx/LeyesBiblio/pdf/LGPDPPSO.pdf.

[16] http://inicio.ifai.org.mx/SitePages/marcoNormativo.aspx?a=acceso.

[17] www.dof.gob.mx/nota_detalle.php?codigo=5382838&fecha=20/02/2015.

[18] www.dof.gob.mx/nota_detalle.php?codigo=5507476&fecha=12/12/2017.

[19] www.diputados.gob.mx/LeyesBiblio/pdf/LFEA.pdf.

[20] http://dof.gob.mx/nota_to_doc.php?codnota=5522133.

[21] http://dof.gob.mx/nota_detalle.php?codigo=5478024&fecha=30/03/2017.

[22] https://www.gob.mx/cms/uploads/attachment/file/271884/Estrategia_Nacional_Ciberseguridad.pdf.

[23] https://www.gob.mx/cidge/estructuras/consejo-ejecutivo-y-consejos-tecnicos.

4 Strides towards a digital and user-driven administration in Mexico

Chapter 4 provides a general overview of the Mexican public administration's capability to successfully implement digital government. It touches upon digital transformation standards and design principles, as well as other tools supporting the emergence of a digital culture in the Mexican public sector. The chapter also delves into the issue of the Mexican's state data capability and concrete ways to foster a data-driven culture in the public sector to improve government performance. This chapter advances an assessment of the key challenges facing Mexico in terms of developing and deploying a digital talent strategy. Chapter 4 closes with considerations about current challenges in deploying new methods for ICT commissioning and acquisition and stresses the need to increasingly adopt agile development approaches.

Digital service transformation

Mexico[1] has joined Australia,[2] Canada,[3] New Zealand,[4] the United Kingdom[5] and the United States[6] in developing design principles, standards, guides and other requirements for digitalisation of public services. This trend has given rise to the internationally recognised Principles for Digital Development[7] and the OECD's forthcoming General Digital Service Design Principles, a document developed by the Thematic Group on Digital Service Delivery of the OECD Working Party of Senior Digital Government Officials. These tools have been powerful tools to boost the digital transformation. They have encouraged digital teams across the administration not to simply digitalise paper-based procedures, but to focus on redesigning them and how to go about it.

By providing digital teams with a principle-based approach to service design, these tools empower teams to leave behind obsolete rules that make little sense. They also provide a clear definition about what good-performing services are, shifting incentives to bring a greater focus on user-driven services (Bracken and Greenway, 2018; Bracken et al., 2018).

Indeed, the power of Mexico's guidelines, standards[8] and principles has been to a great extent magnified by the governance framework put around the government's single portal, Gob.mx (Box 4.1). This has allowed the Digital Government Unit to be able to decide whether something is good enough to go on the portal or not, thus serving as quality control.

Along with the government's Seal of Excellence, a government tool providing incentives for compliance with government guidelines and standards, the framework for digital services has brought Mexico a long way, not only in terms of service transformation, but also in terms of government digital innovation. The government of Mexico has made efforts to build capabilities (within and outside of the public sector) to harness the power of emerging technologies, with a particular focus on artificial intelligence (AI; see next section) and blockchain or distributed ledger technologies (see Box 4.2). The question today is how to move further ahead.

One answer for this is the need for embedding digital leadership and approaches across departments and levels of government. A push coming from the centre can only get you so far and is unlikely to deliver lasting, government-wide cultural transformation. In this sense, it is important to understand that digital leaders are not IT specialists, but individuals who can strategically leverage the power and principles of technologies to achieve their organisations' strategic objectives. In this sense, the title digital transformation officers must go beyond a fancy name, ensuring these officers do not become or rename an IT support system. To help drive change, digital transformation officers should be politically able, and stay close to the ears of organisational boards and become the voice of service users within the organisation (Bracken and Greenway, 2018).

Organisations might also benefit from the presence of chief technology officers (CTOs), individuals able to help organisational leaders navigate the different technological options as these increase in number and become more complex (Bracken and Greenway, 2018). A CTO is expected to clarify the specifics of the options, the trade-offs and their implications. This role is not always the fulfilled by the same person as a digital transformation officer.

> **Box 4.1. Gob.mx: Transforming service delivery and digital engagement in Mexico**
>
> Gob.mx has been at the core of the digital government strategy in Mexico. Developed and tested in the course of 2013 and 2014, the platform has since become the government's single window and an essential shared infrastructure for government transformation. It allows users to easily access services and public information as well as take part in digital participation exercises.
>
> The platform has also facilitated interoperability and data sharing within the public sector, ensured consistency in design, and made government more accessible for citizens and businesses. By mandating that all public institutions participate in the platform, the government of Mexico gave the Coordination of the National Digital Strategy office and the Ministry of Public Administration greater ability to ensure that digital services comply with the technical standards and requirements. These standards and requirements, along with a series of guides, templates and reusable components, have been made available for all public institutions to reuse, helping accelerate the transformation of services.
>
> The three main components of the portal are:
>
> 1. Gob.mx/tramites: gives citizens and business quick, easy access to 4 000 federal public services
> 2. Gob.mx/gobierno: a shared content management system and a UX design standard applied to 5 336 government websites, effectively consolidating, harmonising and integrating the government's digital presence
> 3. Gob.mx/participa: an interactive platform providing citizens with a channel to make proposals, report acts of corruption, and participate in the development of new services and policies.
>
> Source: Gob.mx (2018), "¿Qué es gob.mx?", webpage, https://www.gob.mx/que-es-gobmx-extendido (accessed on 26 October 2018); OECD (2015), "Digital government toolkit: Good practices – National One-Stop Portal Gob.mx", www.oecd.org/gov/mexico-one-stop-portal.pdf (accessed on 26 October 2018); Coordination of the National Digital Strategy (2018), "National Digital Strategy – Project files", unpublished.

Furthermore, as digital governments achieve new levels of maturity, they have been looking for ways to improve their own digital service standards. The United Kingdom, an OECD peer and trend-setter in this domain, is the clearest example. The UK Government Digital Service is working on a revised framework that will focus, among others, on fostering more joined-up approaches rather than simply individual services (Gill, 12 September 2018). This means a greater focus on what the user is ultimately trying to achieve, rather than individual mandates or responsibilities of departments. Mexico would also benefit from a greater focus on the user journey and life events in the mid- to long term as a means to achieving more substantial, user-driven transformation (Box 4.3).

> **Box 4.2. BlockchainHackMX: Building blockchain capability in Mexico**
>
> In 2017, the government of Mexico established a roadmap for building blockchain capability in the public sector and society-wide, including the development of a Mexican blockchain. This entails the development of a public network that would serve as shared infrastructure, supporting developments within and outside of the public sector.
>
> The government of Mexico defined the technology, the network architecture and a preliminary version of its governance model in 2017 and these were then put to test in early 2018.
>
> In 2017, the government of Mexico launched a digital government vertical in the Talent Hackathon Campus Party 2017, inviting developers to innovate in public service delivery using blockchain. The

> winner of the hackathon was the prototype of an app for "Smart Contracts in Public Procurement". This initiative is currently being pursued to be brought to scale and launched once functional.
>
> Furthermore, Mexico has established a Blockchain Advisory Board with experts from industry, civil society, academia and the public sector to advise the government on the development of the public blockchain, the identification of use cases and provide technical assistance. The use cases identified so far include public procurement; certificates of teacher trainings; public property registry; and a single registry of certificates, warehouses and merchandise.
>
> As of the fourth quarter of 2018, a new version of the governance model for blockchain and the mapping of use cases had been opened to public consultation.

The digital transformation not only helps the government of Mexico to better serve domestic users, but citizens and service users abroad as well. According to the Institute of Mexicans Abroad, an agency attached to the Mexican Ministry of Foreign Affairs, 12 million Mexican citizens live in foreign lands, with 97.3% of them in the United States.[9] In addition, the global economy remains highly integrated and foreign investment and trade a critical strategic area for Mexico. Digital technologies can bring the Mexican government closer to these constituents, allowing citizens to access important services remotely and providing investors with an easy entry point for conducting business in the country. Mexico might also benefit from further exploring cross-border services in North America, and other key markets in Europe and Latin America.

A data culture that supports digital strategy and delivery

The digital disruption is the wealth of data and information produced by the ubiquity of digital devices, which increasingly interact with the physical world (i.e. sensors and the Internet of Things). Growing computing power and increasingly sophisticated statistical models and algorithms (i.e. machine learning algorithms, AI) can lead to better public performance and more robust decision making. Mexico has taken significant steps in this direction.

> **Box 4.3. Transforming service delivery in Korea through life-events approaches**
>
> Korea is widely recognised as one of the most advanced countries when it comes to digital and user-driven public administrations. It has achieved this by putting a strong focus on the user's journey and experience and carrying out a comprehensive implementation of a life-events approach.
>
> As an illustration, the figure below represents the transformation of the administrative procedures required by heirs when confronted with the death of their parents. Prior to the integration of systems, the mourning heir had to complete seven different procedures, including: register the death at his/her local government; provide information on transactions to financial agencies; pay national and local taxes; and complete the transfer of car and lands. These administrative burdens made the mourning even more burdensome. Today, these procedures can be completed with a single form thanks to the integration and interoperability of systems.
>
> Figure 4.1. The transformation of the administrative procedures required by heirs when confronted with the death of their parents
>
>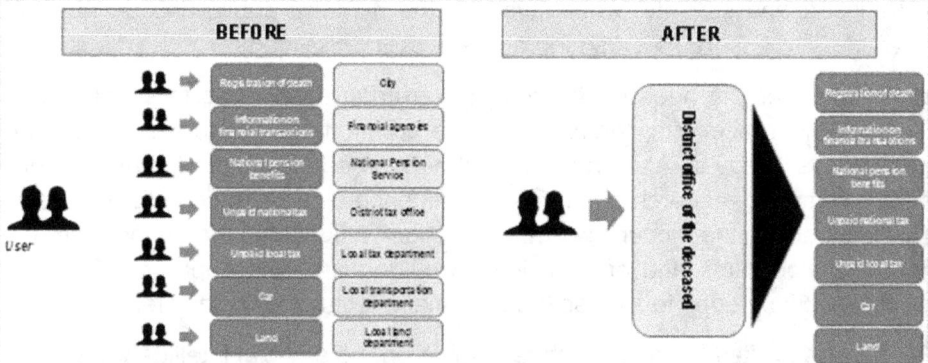
>
> Similarly, today new parents can automatically apply for a wide variety of birth related welfare services using a single form when registering the birth of their baby. This is a tangible example of how services can be reorganised around the user's needs by cutting across traditional silos and areas of responsibility.
>
> Source: Ministry of Interior of Korea (2017), "Presentation at the OECD-MENA Working Group II on Open and Innovative Government".

The government of Mexico has embedded the relevance of data for the digital transformation in the National Digital Strategy (Government of Mexico, 2013), and has made concrete efforts to build the institutional, social and economic infrastructure around it to support it (OECD, 2016; 2018b). Furthermore, it has progressively built the necessary institutional capabilities and the organisational underpinnings to achieve increasing levels of sophistication in the use of data in the public sector. Efforts such as the institutionalisation of chief data officers and digital transformation officers are of remarkable importance to advancing the data operations of the public sector (OECD, 2018b).

Mexico has also maintained a healthy interest in disruptive emerging data-processing technologies that will upend industries, such as AI. Indeed, the government of Mexico is expected to show leadership in this area of critical importance for its sustained economic development. The Coordination of the National Digital Strategy office worked with the British Embassy in Mexico, Oxford Insights and C Minds to develop a white paper that laid out a roadmap for effective and ethical AI in the country (Dutton, 2018; Martinho Truswell et al., 2018), which would then come to be acknowledged as a national policy (Zapata, 22 March 2018).

This policy or strategy looks specifically into the application of AI to government services and administration, R&D, skills and capability, data and digital infrastructure, and the ethics around AI. Following the adoption of the AI strategy, the government of Mexico has pushed for the creation of ia2030, a multi-sectoral partnership to set the course for AI development in the country. This partnership has prepared and put forward for public consultation a proposal of General Principles for the Development and Use of Artificial Intelligence in the Federal Public Administration and a Guide for Impact Assessment in the Development and Use of Systems based on AI in the federal public administration.[10] This is consistent with trends across OECD countries. France, for instance, recently presented the Villani Report, which sets a vision and a strategic approach for the country (Box 4.4).

Box 4.4. France: The Villani Report

The Villani Report, published in March 2018, offers a series of recommendations to ensure that artificial intelligence (AI) generates the best possible benefits in the French society and economy. Among the different aspects covered, the report discusses the importance of defining a French data policy and creating a French AI ecosystem in order to enable and promote the application of AI in the country. It also indicates that efforts in terms of artificial intelligence need to focus on four main areas (health, environment, transport and security) while involving the different public and private stakeholders of those respective fields to ensure AI is used to address policy challenges.

The report also addresses the need for a strong government leadership to spearhead the impact of artificial intelligence in France with, for example, the creation of an inter-ministerial co ordinator to implement the French strategy on AI. Furthermore, the report advocates for the need to provide training programmes and promoting research on artificial intelligence as well as establishing clear ethics for AI and assessing its impact on the labour market. In addition, it highlights the importance of transparency in machine-learning algorithms and of adopting an evidence-based approach; for instance, testing projects targeting specific groups to assess the potential effects of artificial intelligence.

The Villani Report was drafted by the French task force on the artificial intelligence strategy for France and Europe, which was created in September 2017 by the French Prime Minister.

The task force was composed of different stakeholders from academia and the French Digital Council, and it received the assistance of the French Secretary of State for Digital Affairs and other government institutions. Its mission began in September 2017 and ended in March 2018, with different hearings, public consultations and surveys that were held.

Source: OECD with information from Villani, C. (2018), "For a meaningful artificial intelligence: Towards a French and European strategy", https://www.aiforhumanity.fr/pdfs/MissionVillani_Report_ENG-VF.pdf (accessed on 26 October 2018).

In this regard, and as discussed in Chapter 2, Mexico has largely succeeded in making the case for the relevance of open data and data-driven approaches going forward. The question now is how to nurture a data-driven culture in the public sector that is ingrained in public sector operations and strategic priorities and policy objectives.

One of the first challenges in achieving this once awareness has been raised is ensuring that public organisations have the ability to look beyond the hype and engage with a way of thinking that is founded on a thorough understanding of technologies' opportunities, but also understanding their limitations and what they cannot achieve. A clear-eyed view that understands that data are not about buzz, but about taking better decisions, and deploys data capabilities consequently. Data science skills are scarce and expensive. Public sector resources should be used with balanced understanding of their power, but also of the scarcity of these resources if it intends to achieve maximum impact.

Effective use of data starts with determining the business or policy problem an organisation would like to solve. The problems and strategic questions, not the hype, should drive the data efforts in the public sector (Díaz, Rowshankish and Saleh, 2018). Data analytics have been successfully deployed in digital service delivery through the Gob.mx portal, but cases of successful implementation for policy making are still scarce. As such, the data governance in the Mexican federal public administration should continue to encourage and expand the implementation of data-driven techniques in highly strategic ways through frameworks, incentives, guidance and capacity building.

While frameworks and systems are critical, culture ultimately relies on people and are preserved by senior leadership. Technological disruption is not new, but what makes the digital age unique is its pace, scope and reach. Political leaders and senior management in public institutions are still only rarely digital natives, but as mentioned in the previous chapter, the speed and depth of technological change exposes them to great risk of failure if they do not understand the strategic implications of these changes and of the choices in front of them (Díaz, Rowshankish and Saleh, 2018).

To strategically deploy efforts in advanced analytics and other data-processing innovations, public sector leadership does not have a choice but to take the time to grasp these technologies, how they could change or shape their operating environment, what opportunities they bring, and what risk they entail. As previously mentioned, this outcome will demand direct and frequent lines of communications between chief data officers and digital transformation officers and the top decision makers in the organisation. This will also empower these digital and data officers by giving them the opportunity to bring technology and data to bear as valuable sources of evidence to inform strategic decisions and to support policy implementation to achieve policy objectives. As top-level decision makers progressively see how technology and data can make them more effective executives, this relationship is bound to gain the digital and data-driven culture support.

Ultimately, to embed a data-driven culture into the fabric of the state, regardless of changing administrations, chief data officers and data scientists must be able to work effectively with business units and operations. By making the latter improve the delivery of their respective functions, thus enhancing the performance of these units, chief data officers and their teams will gain growing support and interest from the different parts of the organisation.

The Mexican public sector would also benefit from focusing early data-driven missions to improve public sector performance in areas that require substantial effort, thus ensuring high returns on investment. For instance, predictive maintenance of infrastructure and equipment could lead to substantial savings of resources and lives (Bender, Henke and Lamarre, 2018).

The interest from business units in different sectors of the administration should be nurtured with the secured and free flow of data within the organisation, unless justified for legitimate privacy or security concerns. The free flow of data will become an increasingly important complement for the progressive spread of data and analytics capabilities across the public sector. If developed within the right framework, the growing interest in data-driven approaches from across the Mexican public administration will likely result in exponential benefits from data-driven innovations while ensuring that solutions are interoperable, compliant and ethical. Ideally, data governance frameworks and data infrastructures should help advance data accessibility, usability and sharing. These frameworks should also be conducive to growing robustness in data quality and reliability, and promote the continuous enrichment of data for it to be made more valuable and easily exploited. Mexico should concentrate on maintaining the focus on setting the right data policy framework covering all key aspects of the data governance for value creation as to maximise the potential of national data value chains. If the government of Mexico achieves this, it will be ready to reap the benefits of digitalisation as the prospects of machine learning and AI applications in the public sector come closer to reality. More importantly, Mexico will be on a high-speed rail to a digital, proactive, data- and user-driven administration.

Figure 4.2. Data governance in the public sector

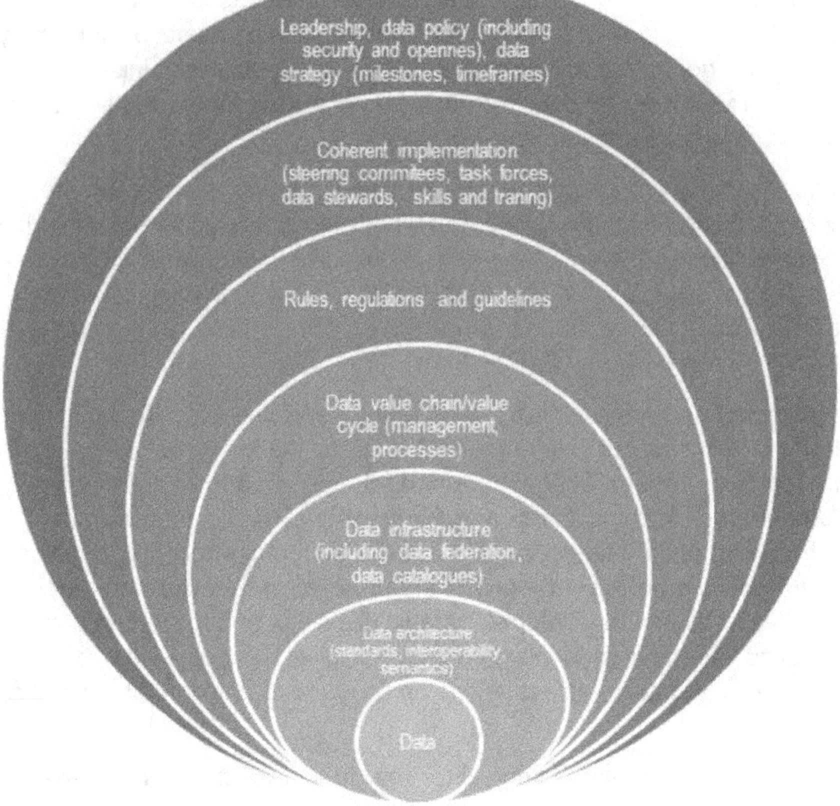

(Concentric circles, from outermost to innermost:)
- Leadership, data policy (including security and openness), data strategy (milestones, timeframes)
- Coherent implementation (steering committees, task forces, data stewards, skills and training)
- Rules, regulations and guidelines
- Data value chain/value cycle (management, processes)
- Data infrastructure (including data federation, data catalogues)
- Data architecture (standards, interoperability, semantics)
- Data

Source: OECD (forthcoming), Digital Government Review of Sweden.

Building digital capability in the Mexican public sector

As highlighted in the previous chapter, digital reform ultimately comes down to the human factor. Government transformation is first and foremost about transforming the way government works and building new capabilities and a culture that supports delivery.

Digitalisation will transform the future of work, requiring new skills in every sector and industry (Chui, Manyika and Miremadi, 2015; Manyika et al., 2017). Government is not an exception. Quite the contrary, decades of outsourcing IT delivery and maintenance has probably undermined the public sector's ability to manage and deliver IT projects, not to mention digital design and delivery approaches. The Mexican public sector faces the need to deploy strategies to reskill, upskill and acquire new talent in the public sector in order to deliver on its digital ambitions.

The government of Mexico has shown awareness about this issue, which lead to the launching of its new Digital Academy,[11] a platform providing civil servants access to online courses. It also provides guidance on how to obtain access to in-person digital government training workshops organised by the Digital Government Unit of the Ministry of Public Administration. While this is an important first step in upskilling civil servants, these activities do not have the scope or scale needed to respond to the challenge of the digital transformation.

It is important for the Mexican public sector to clearly differentiate between the skills that it may need to acquire and the capabilities it can build internally with existing staff. Project managers and other roles can be retrained to identify digital opportunities and use agile or DevOps methodologies instead of waterfall project management relatively easy. However, areas like data science, machine learning, artificial intelligence or even human-centred design require very specific skills, backgrounds and experience which are hard to transfer (Bughin et al., 2018). In addition, talent in these areas is scarce and in high demand, but very much needed for a successful digital transformation.

Mexico might benefit from a strategy to quickly attract new digital talent to the public sector while these new skills become more available and are able to spread more broadly across the public sector. These skills are, however, needed to respond to digital challenges today. For this, it would have to work to choose better candidates and make public sector employment or missions more attractive for these highly skilled individuals.

First of all, it should take a comprehensive look at public sector human resource and compensation policies to enable the public sector to manage talent effectively and revise and streamline its public employment frameworks to ensure that the hiring process is more agile and candidates are tested for the relevant abilities. As such, a data scientist should not be asked to write eloquent essays, nor be judged on the basis of his CV or interview alone. Candidates for a position as a data scientist should be asked to perform relevant tasks for the job, including data mining, processing massive amounts of data or setting up data collection techniques for a given service (Bracken and Greenway, 2018; Bracken et al., 2018). Furthermore, these candidates should be assessed by a panel of technical experts that can provide a robust assessment of the candidate's actual knowledge and capabilities.

In addition, roles should be clearly defined and titles shouldn't be used loosely. If public organisations call any data role a data scientist, the value and prestige that comes with the title will erode, making it harder to attract talent from the private sector. Moreover, public institutions and managers may end up being even more confused about who they are or should be hiring and to do what. Countries like the United Kingdom have taken a proactive stance in this domain and have been setting up competency frameworks for key digital and data positions as well as clarifying the role and responsibilities of these positions in the civil service.[12] The federal public administration could also aim to make the public sector more attractive to digital talent by reviewing compensation frameworks to allow for performance-based bonuses and to appropriately recognise, price and compensate scarce talent.

Box 4.5. Attracting new talent in government in the United States

After the 2011 Healthcare.gov debacle, it became evident that the US federal government had to drastically change how it procured and managed IT projects. While public sector wages weren't as competitive in the public sector, the US federal government was able to develop a strategy to attract digital talent from the vibrant tech industry building on tech entrepreneurs' and specialists' interest in having a social impact at a scale that only the federal government could offer.

Indeed, the Obama administration succeeded in creating a series of programmes that called upon highly skilled software engineers to perform missions of six months to two years to tackle specific problems. These missions were framed as civic duties that would ultimately enhance government performance and its ability to use technology to deliver better services, even if such efforts would be hard to sustain in the long term unless they transformed the practices of career civil servants (Mergel, 2017; OECD, 2018a).

Sources: Mergel, I. (2017), "Digital service teams: Challenges and recommendations for government", http://dx.doi.org/10.13140/RG.2.2.27227.57121; OECD (2018a), Digital Government Review of Morocco: Laying the Foundations for the Digital Transformation of the Public Sector in Morocco, https://doi.org/10.1787/9789264298729-en.

Another key area of improvement as Mexico seeks to build its capabilities to deliver digital services is the revision of ICT acquisition frameworks to support more integrated and digital delivery.

Through the ICT Policy,[13] its implementation guides and handbooks,[14] the government of Mexico has established a clear process for conducting an ICT commissioning exercise and structuring ICT projects. These include basic requirements, such as the use of open standards, reusable components, digital identity, meeting interoperability requirements. In addition, the current policy is sound in identifying a project manager, establishing ICT project catalogues, performing feasibility studies, structuring a business case and providing clear definitions of minimum requirements. These specifications are made more robust by the use of the Digital Government Seal of Excellence,[15] granted to those services that meet the existing digital government standards and have gone through a robust process of development. This tool serves as a strong incentive for compliance with digital government standards, norms and guidelines.

To make procurement simpler, the government of Mexico has also set up framework agreements for software licensing with 31 software providers.[16] Moreover, the government is currently developing a software framework agreement to efficiently respond to the software needs of public organisations.[17] While these efforts are greatly valuable as they save the public sector time and resources, more can be done to expand the number of providers participating in this sort of agreement, to limit concentration and expand the pool of providers to the state. Ultimately, 31 firms are just too few to ensure adequate competition among providers and licensing agreements are not enough to respond to the need more tailored solutions.

Procurement frameworks and business cases would also benefit from clarifying the approach and contracting modalities to facilitate the use of agile methodologies, contracting approaches and project structures are aligned with digital service standards and design principles. The ICT Policy asks project managers to define service requirements and functionalities in advance. This is sensible, but it should be recognised that the need for new functionalities and requirements may and will be revealed in the testing or roll out stages, requiring further iteration and improvement. While the digital standard and the service design principles of the government of Mexico provide guidance to project managers on how to manage digitalisation initiatives, the ICT Policy and handbook do not clearly advise on how to conduct the procurement process or structure contracts to effectively use agile approaches.

If not carefully structured, contracts may require successive extensions to address problems with the solutions delivered, improve functionality or user experience, which may be uneconomical and inefficient. As Mexico's design principles highlight, experience shows that digital services should privilege agile approaches, which enables the organisation to work on frequent iterations or improvements. As such, the underlining frameworks, such as business cases and procurement frameworks, do not do project managers a service if either by action or omission they push managers to structure the project as a traditional waterfall initiative where all the specifics and functionalities of the digital solutions are determined in advance, without user input. 18F, inside the General Services Administration, developed agile purchasing agreements that made agile contracting easier for the whole federal administration of the United States (Box 4.6).

> **Box 4.6. 18F's agile procurement agreements in the United States**
>
> 18F, an innovative digital transformation team within the US General Services Administration made up of top-notch talent coming mainly from the tech industry, has looked at introducing new technology deployment techniques in the US federal government. To do so, they have developed new contract and service agreement templates that are compatible with agile software development.
>
> As part of this effort, 18F established the agile blanket purchase agreements, which radically transform the ICT procurement approach. Instead of traditional requests for proposals, which require very detailed descriptions of technical requirements and specifications in advance – by definition unlikely to include all the functionalities and details the contractor would like to include, as the testing and use process most often reveals – blanket purchase agreements work as a competition that requires participating firms to prepare a prototype in an open GitHub repository open for everybody to see. This approach allows the contractor to appreciate what competing firms are actually able to deliver. The blanket purchase agreements can foresee agile development sprints and iterations, allowing both the contractor and the service provider to progressively define software requirements and functionalities as the project advances.
>
> Source: Mergel, I. (2017), "Digital service teams: Challenges and recommendations for government", http://dx.doi.org/10.13140/RG.2.2.27227.57121.

Furthermore, investment and funding frameworks and cycles can support iterative digitalisation projects, in particular for large projects. Funding can be progressively disbursed based on a results assessment of project stages (i.e. Alpha, Beta, roll out). This strengthens the governance of large projects and enables a progressive learning process for project managers. It also limits the risks of large IT investments by conditioning funding on delivery. These frameworks, however, require the sound use of project thresholds to structure the governance of IT projects.

Moreover, IT project management frameworks and guidance might benefit from encouraging practitioners to adopt more joined-up management approaches, such as DevOps. The DevOps model (development and operations) brings together a combination of philosophies, practices and tools (including agile) to achieve greater integration of development and operations in ICT projects to deliver applications and services more quickly. This approach seeks to break down the silos between the development and business units or operations teams to evolve products faster.[18] As Mexico seeks to achieve greater digital integration in its public sector, these approaches are well worth the investment.

References

Bender, M., N. Henke and E. Lamarre (2018), "The cornerstones of large-scale technology transformation", McKinsey Quarterly, October, https://www.mckinsey.com/business-functions/digital-mckinsey/our-insights/the-cornerstones-of-large-scale-technology-transformation.

Bracken, M. and Greenway, A. (2018), How to Achieve and Sustain Government Digital Transformation, Inter-American Development Bank, Washington, DC, http://dx.doi.org/10.18235/0001215.

Bracken, M. et al. (2018), Digital Transformation at Scale: Why the Strategy is Delivery, London Publishing Partnership, London.

Bughin, J. et al. (2018), "Why digital strategies fail", McKinsey Quarterly, January, https://www.mckinsey.com/business-functions/digital-mckinsey/our-insights/why-digital-strategies-fail.

Chui, M., J. Manyika and M. Miremadi (2015), "Four fundamentals of workplace automation", McKinsey Quarterly, November, https://www.mckinsey.com/business-functions/digital-mckinsey/our-insights/four-fundamentals-of-workplace-automation.

Coordination of the National Digital Strategy (2018), "National Digital Strategy – Project files", unpublished.

Díaz, A., K. Rowshankish and T. Saleh (2018), "Why data culture matters", McKinsey Quarterly, September, https://www.mckinsey.com/business-functions/mckinsey-analytics/our-insights/why-data-culture-matters.

Dutton, T. (2018), "Artificial intelligence strategies", Medium.com - Politics + AI.

Gill, S. (12 September 2018), "What's happening with the service standard?", Government Digital Service blog, https://gds.blog.gov.uk/2018/09/12/whats-happening-with-the-service-standard.

Gob.mx (2018), "¿Qué es gob.mx?", webpage, https://www.gob.mx/que-es-gobmx-extendido (accessed on 26 October 2018).

Government of Mexico (2013), Estrategia Digital Nacional, Presidencia de los Estados Unidos Mexicanos.

Manyika, J. et al. (2017), "Jobs lost, jobs gained: What the future of work will mean for jobs, skills, and wages", McKinsey Global Institute, https://www.mckinsey.com/~/media/McKinsey/Featured%20Insights/Future%20of%20Organizations/What%20the%20future%20of%20work%20will%20mean%20for%20jobs%20skills%20and%20wages/MGI-Jobs-Lost-Jobs-Gained-Report-December-6-2017.ashx.

Martinho-Truswell, E. et al. (2018), "Towards an AI strategy in Mexico: Harnessing the AI revolution", White Paper, British Embassy Mexico City, Oxford Insights and C Minds.

Mergel, I. (2017), "Digital service teams: Challenges and recommendations for government", IBM Center for the Business of Government, Washington, DC, http://dx.doi.org/10.13140/RG.2.2.27227.57121.

Ministry of Interior of Korea (2017), "Presentation at the OECD-MENA Working Group II on Open and Innovative Government", Dubai, United Arab Emirates, February.

OECD (forthcoming), Digital Government Review of Sweden: Enabling Government as a Platform through a Data-Driven Public Sector, OECD Publishing, Paris, forthcoming.

OECD (2018a), Digital Government Review of Morocco: Laying the Foundations for the Digital Transformation of the Public Sector in Morocco, OECD Publishing, Paris, https://doi.org/10.1787/9789264298729-en.

OECD (2018b), Open Government Data in Mexico: The Way Forward, OECD Publishing, Paris, https://doi.org/10.1787/9789264297944-en.

OECD (2016), Open Government Data Review of Mexico: Data Reuse for Public Sector Impact and Innovation, OECD Publishing, Paris, https://doi.org/10.1787/9789264259270-en.

OECD (2015), "Digital government toolkit: Good practices – National One-Stop Portal Gob.mx", OECD, Paris, www.oecd.org/gov/mexico-one-stop-portal.pdf (accessed on 26 October 2018).

Villani, C. (2018), "For a meaningful artificial intelligence: Towards a French and European strategy", French Task Force on Artificial Intelligence, Paris, https://www.aiforhumanity.fr/pdfs/MissionVillani_Report_ENG-VF.pdf (accessed on 26 October 2018)

Zapata, E. (22 March 2018), "Estrategia de inteligencia artificial MX 2018, Gob.mx", México Digital Blog, https://www.gob.mx/mexicodigital/articulos/estrategia-de-inteligencia-artificial-mx-2018.

Notes

[1] Mexican digital service design principles, https://www.gob.mx/serviciosdigitales/articulos/principios-generales-de-diseno-de-servicios-digitales; digital service standard and reusable tools, https://www.gob.mx/estandar; guides, https://www.gob.mx/wikiguias.

[2] https://www.dta.gov.au/standard.

[3] https://www.canada.ca/en/government/publicservice/modernizing/government-canada-digital-standards.html.

[4] https://www.digital.govt.nz/standards-and-guidance/digital-service-design-standard.

[5] https://www.gov.uk/service-manual/service-standard.

[6] https://playbook.cio.gov.

[7] https://digitalprinciples.org.

[8] https://www.gob.mx/estandar.

[9] www.ime.gob.mx/gob/estadisticas/2016/mundo/estadistica_poblacion.html.

[10] https://www.gob.mx/participa/consultas/principiosiamx.

[11] https://www.gob.mx/academiadigital.

[12] https://www.gov.uk/government/collections/digital-data-and-technology-profession-capability-framework.

[13] https://www.gob.mx/cms/uploads/attachment/file/380408/MAAGTICSI_compilado__20182208.pdf.

[14] https://www.gob.mx/cms/uploads/attachment/file/32502/Guia-CUTIC.pdf.

[15] www.dof.gob.mx/nota_detalle.php?codigo=5446678&fecha=03/08/2016.

[16] https://www.gob.mx/sfp/documentos/contrato-marco-licencias-de-software.

[17] https://www.gob.mx/sfp/documentos/contrato-marco-software?state=published.

[18] https://aws.amazon.com/devops/what-is-devops.